BROKEN TO
B.O.L.D

Broken to Bold: A Journey of a Rise to the Top, a Major Fall and a Revelation of Truth.

Copyright © 2020 *Kelly Kennedy*

All rights reserved. No part of this book may be used or reproduced by any means, graphic, electronic, mechanical, including photocopying, recording, taping, or by any information storage retrieval system without the written permission of the author except in the case of brief quotations embodied in critical articles and reviews.

Scriptures taken from the Holy Bible, New International Version®, NIV®. Copyright © 1973, 1978, 1984, 2011 by Biblica, Inc.™ Used by permission of Zondervan. All rights reserved worldwide. www.zondervan.com The "NIV" and "New International Version" are trademarks registered in the United States Patent and Trademark Office by Biblica, Inc.™

ISBN: 9798550558003

A Publication of Tall Pine Books

|| *tallpinebooks.com*

*Printed in the United States of America

BROKEN TO
BOLD

THE JOURNEY OF A RISE TO THE TOP, A MAJOR FALL,
AND A REVELATION OF TRUTH.

KELLY KENNEDY

TALL PINE

This book is dedicated to my husband, Todd, for his unconditional love and support. My love, you have stood by me through every crazy idea I have had and especially in the writing of this book. I am so grateful for you. To my lovely daughters, Molly, Finley and Caitlin: You have taught me more about how to teach and coach with more love and compassion, understanding and encouragement than anybody. Thank you for loving me through my intense coaching days and teaching me how to be a better coach, and for your support and encouragement in writing this book. You are all amazing and I am forever thankful and blessed to be your wife and mom.

Contents

Preface	ix
Introduction	xiii
1. Pregame Warm-ups	1
2. My Coaching Journey	9
3. Post-Coaching Realities	33
4. The Long Road To Healing	49
5. The X's and O's of Success	77
6. Coaching Is A Challenge At Every Level	103
7. Life Lessons	143
Epilogue	163
Overtime	169
Acknowledgments	179
Meet the Author	181
Endnotes	183

Preface

Thank you.

By picking up this book you have entrusted me with your most precious possession—your time—so I am going to talk to you as a friend in a most intimate conversation. In the pages that follow, I am going to be raw and real with you. I have been told that the greatest way for people to trust you is to be real and vulnerable with them. My hope is that it might help you to drop your guard and be vulnerable as well.

Many friends have encouraged me to write a book, but I've never felt qualified. What could I possibly have to say to someone that would help them move forward in their life?

Although we had struggles while I was growing up inside our home, on the outside things looked pretty good for me. Life just seemed to fall in place for me, and I seemed to have success wherever I went. I got good grades, I was on student-council, I was picked in the top four for every kickball game in the school yard (even by the boys).

But, behind all this surface "success" was brokenness. Everyone has their own brokenness they hide, and we all find ways to conceal it as long as things are going well. It's when the wheels start to wobble and eventually fall off that the brokenness is exposed. What happens then? Do we crumble in a heap or dust ourselves off and move forward? I guess that all depends on what you make the source of strength in your life. I want to show you how I found a source of strength that I trust and put it to work in a positive way.

It is not easy to begin, especially when it involves getting real about your own failures and shortcomings. The darkness that I had to humbly walk through to get to this point resulted in many tears of pain and then of joy.

Pain is a part of our life journeys; there is a purpose for it, whether we like it or not. Jesus suffered for us to have eternal life. Our suffering is to help us to grow closer to Jesus, to relate to what He went through for us, and to renew us—to chisel away at the surface and go deeper into who the Creator designed us to be. We are all "called according to His purpose," but it is up to us to accept the call.

As my good friend and mentor, Tom Roy told me, "you have to walk through the pain so that you can use it to help others." I initially got into coaching because I wanted to help kids, so that made sense to me. If this book helps to liberate a fellow coach to be free to live out his/her life according to God's plan and for His glory, then the risk is worth it. My pain is His tool; I am simply the messenger.

Through God's grace and love I have found the truth. Jesus said, "The truth shall make you free." The peace and joy in knowing God and experiencing that freedom through His great love are priceless. If you are going through a tough time, I pray that you find something in these pages that helps you in your healing process. It's important to remember that healing is a process, not an event. If you are willing to dig deeply into the root of the pain, you can find freedom and peace, and welcome the Spirit of the Lord into the process with you. Where the Spirit of the Lord is, there is Freedom.

I have been marvelously ruined by the love of God and have found peace in His love. I have applied this to my coaching since I learned that it's not about winning, but about the positive impact we get to make in young peoples' lives as we walk out God's love in our coaching. I sometimes wish I had come to this realization while I was still a collegiate coach, but here we are. God has a plan for each of us. He uses the broken to heal the hurting. I hope my reflections on my rise and fall as a coach will help you, whatever stage of the game you are currently in, and that you will put these truths into practice... like, literally, into your practice.

Coaches know what I'm talking about.

"You called me out upon the waters,
The great unknown where feet may fail,
And there I find You in the mystery
In oceans deep my faith will stand."
— From "Oceans" by Hillsong

In 2017, I was blessed to go to Israel, where I floated on the Sea of Galilee. You may recognize the Sea of Galilee as the scene of the most famous example of walking on water. There, my Heavenly Father confirmed His love for me as His precious child. He knows my heart and my desires. The fact that my most peaceful place to be in life is in a boat on the water. It is no coincidence that He most fully revealed His love to me on water. This book is a testimony to His grace and mercy and love that will forever guide my life.

"And I wish you to know, brothers (and sisters), that what has befallen me has turned out for the advancement of the Good News, so that it has become known to all the rest, that my chains are for Jesus Christ, and most of the brothers (and sisters), trusting in the Messiah because of my chains, are much more bold to fearlessly speak the word." (Philippians 1: 12-14)

In writing this book, I have grown deeper in my faith and trust in my Heavenly Father through the unwavering love of His Son, Jesus, my Savior. I have dug further into the Word of God, growing deeper in my understanding of His love for me. I have seen the manifestation of Romans 8:28: "And we know that ALL MATTERS work together for good for those who love Elohim (God's name in Hebrew), to those who are called according to His purpose" through my struggles.

I want to give all glory to God as the author of my story. He gave me the boldness to speak out about the goodness of His love from the brokenness of my failures.

Introduction

My 18-month-old daughter, Molly was in the back seat of my car as I drove home in the pouring rain from James A. Rhodes Arena at the University of Akron. It had been another tumultuous day at work: my staff was a mess, I was a mess, and the tension was as thick as the crowding fog around me. I felt like such a failure. Molly sighed as she stared out the window at the rain. As I glanced at her in the mirror, I felt the piercing sting of wanting to be a good mom, whatever that meant, and sensing that I was failing at that, too. I really had hit rock bottom, with nowhere to turn.

On the radio, Carrie Underwood was belting out, "Jesus, take the wheel." It was then that I surrendered myself, crying out for Jesus to take the wheel. I didn't know what I was going to do next, but at that point, it didn't seem to matter. Anything had to be better than what I was going through at that moment.

Little did I know where that prayer would lead me.

A month later, I found myself in a meeting with the new Athletic Director. I had only met with him once since he came on board, but I felt good about him and confidently walked in his office. But the door was barely closed when I was totally blind-sided. "You will no longer be the coach at Akron," he intoned calmly. "We are asking you to resign or be fired, it's your choice."

I never saw this coming. The words hung in the slow-motion silence as I took them in. Suddenly, anger slapped me back into real time. Outrage poured in behind it, followed by shame and embarrassment. I felt the waters rising around me. Everything I knew about myself and my career was being stripped away by this complete stranger.

Back at home, my husband, Todd stood silently as I unloaded my new reality all over the kitchen. Gripped with pain, shame, and anger, I doubled over. I struggled to catch my breath as I relived those dark moments. "What am I going to do?" I shouted, "I am a coach! That is who I am, and he just took that away from me. I didn't do anything wrong to deserve this." I am sure many other choice words flew out of my mouth.

I had built my whole identity in being a NCAA Division I College Basketball Coach. I did not know what to do without it. I rose fairly quickly up the "ladder" of success to reach the head coaching position. I had not faced adversity like this in my coaching career. I was young and confident and felt bullet proof – until this. Denial was the first voice to speak, and it came easily—denying that I had any responsibility for their decision was easier than accepting the shame that hung around me. I chalked it up to, "we got a new Athletic Director and he wanted to 'go in a different direction,' to get one of his friends into that position."

It took me eight years to finally admit that I was fired. Mind you, I did not sit idly by and sulk. My personality would have never allowed that.

I grew up a hard-working kid. I credit my parents with instilling in me the realization that you have to work for what you want. It was all I knew. For example, when I was ten years old, I really wanted a new bicycle. I had a bike that Santa brought me when I was eight, the old "Star Spangler" with the American flag on the banana seat. But I had my eye on this really cool ten- speed Schwinn. Since I had a bike that worked perfectly fine, replacing it was out of the question. If I wanted THAT bike, I had to work for it. So, every morning before school my brother and I would get up and walk across Lakeshore Boulevard to deliver newspapers. We would walk door to door, putting the paper wherever the customer requested. It was a lot for a ten-year-old, but the dream of riding that new ten-speed kept me getting up early every morning.

Now, that driven, self-motivated side of me that had served me so well in my career was driving me to chase new trophies. I needed to be actively pursuing something; to be my own boss. Business success fueled my ego, made me feel like a winner again. It helped me mute the voices of shame and disgrace. Plus, it promised new channels to make more money. Because, of course, making more money solves all problems, right?

I got involved in multi-level marketing, which promises all kinds of wealth and rewards. My mentor told me, "Kelly, if you want to make more money, you need to grow." All I heard was "make more money," and I was in. I was going to blow the lid off this thing and reap rewards for a lifetime. I was going to show them all how it was done...or so I thought. That competitive nature was firing up inside of me. I want to win at anything I do.

In April 2014, Todd and I went to a business development seminar...at least that's what I thought it was. The presenter challenged the 1,000 people in the room: "How do you answer to your boss?" I don't remember if I meant to say it out loud, or just to myself, but I blurted out, "What if you don't have a boss?" The presenter wheeled around to me and dropped a bomb I will never forget: "that's your first problem." I sat in stunned silence, letting the words sink in.

Then it hit me, and I was brought to my knees: I needed a boss. More accurately, I needed to accept "The BOSS" in my life. Since that moment, I have been on a mission to know and honor my boss, my Heavenly Father.

That session of the seminar was followed by a time of reflection. During this quiet time, the song "Oceans," by Hillsong UNITED, was playing. These lyrics spoke to me so deeply:

> You call me out upon the waters
> The great unknown where feet may fail
> And there I find You in the mystery
> In oceans deep
> My faith will stand
> And I will call upon Your name
> And keep my eyes above the waves
> When oceans rise, my soul will rest in Your embrace
> For I am Yours and You are mine
> Your grace abounds in deepest waters
> Your sovereign hand
> Will be my guide
> Where feet may fail and fear surrounds me
> You've never failed and You won't start now
> So I will call upon Your name
> And keep my eyes above the waves
> When oceans rise, my soul will rest in Your embrace
> For I am Yours and You are mine
> Spirit lead me where my trust is without border
> Let me walk upon the waters
> Wherever You would call me
> Take me deeper than my feet could ever wander

*And my faith will be made stronger
In the presence of my Savior."* [1]

I was being called out upon the waters, out of the depths of my hurting past. There is a quote that comes to mind: "as you look back on your experiences, that is where you truly learn and grow." Through the years of coaching and then business ownership, I have had many experiences that challenged me to learn and grow. I want to share with you the lessons I have learned and dig down into the depths of what they meant for me, to help you to become the person you want to be. If I can, I want to help you avoid the pitfalls I slipped into.

My identity was so entrenched in what I did as a coach, that I couldn't get my head above water. And so my eyes were opened and the journey began to get to know my Heavenly Father and learn about His love for me and who I truly am: a daughter of the Most High God. I have spent the last several years focused on learning, understanding, and growing in that love and all that this meant for me, and now I want to share what it can mean for you too.

1

Pregame Warm-ups

I WAS BORN on Pearl Harbor Day, December 7, 1970. I always would say that my Mom "got a bang" out of me. As the youngest of 10 kids (7 boys and 3 girls), I had to find humor in life. I was a bit of a pistol, but I had to be to survive. There are 17 years difference between my oldest sister, Annie and me.

The Baby of the Family

Annie loved having a baby sister. In fact, so much that she would tell me she was my mom. She would scoop me up with my brother, Keith, and take us on adventures in her little VW bug. We always had fun with our big sis (or was it my mom?). She sure had me believing it for a long time.

Being in a big family had advantages and disadvantages. The bad thing is that I had to wait until I was six when Annie got married and moved out to finally get out of sleeping in a crib. I moved into her room to share with my sister, Kathy. With a nine-year gap between us, we had very different interests and needs. She was in high school and stayed up studying a lot. I had to learn to sleep through anything.

I had some crazy brothers. When I was 4, my brother, Dolphie "kidnapped" Keith and me, and took us to hang out at school for the weekend. I don't remember a whole lot, but it was fun getting all that attention from him and his friends.

Jim, Steve and Stan were off at college for most of the time I can remember. Jimmy likes to tell stories about me when I was little, claiming that he was my favorite. For example, all the kids would get in a circle and put me in the middle. They would all call my name to see who I would come to...who was the favorite? Jimmy claims it was ALWAYS him.

My brother, Mike, was the stud athlete—the one the girls all loved. He was good at everything he did, from baseball to wrestling and popularity: everything I hoped to be when I grew up. I was so excited when he wanted to help coach my t-ball team: a cool teenage brother coaching me; how awesome! And then I realized it was because he had a crush on my friend's sister, who was also coaching. Typical teenage brother!

Most of my memories involve playing sports with the younger brothers. Mike was seven years older than me, and Max was five years older than me and very protective. He liked to embarrass me, too: like the time he and his girlfriend showed up at my first dance in seventh grade. Talk about wanting to die!

Keith and I were the youngest—only 15 months apart. We were often mistaken for twins growing up. We spent a lot of time together, and had as many battles as any other siblings, but we had a lot of fun together, and we looked out for each other. Like the time I snuck him food when he was hiding under the bed, playing hooky in kindergarten. Dad made him change schools and he didn't want to go. I had to look out for my buddy. That relationship has stayed strong to this day. He even stood up as the "man of honor" in my wedding (in the place of a "maid of honor"). I was nice, though: I didn't make him wear a dress.

Anger Breaks Up A Home

Dad had anger issues and it came out in fits of rage at mom and the older siblings. I've come to realize why, once they got out of the house, they didn't come around a whole lot. Home tended to be a war zone. Getting out of the house to go play all day was the best solution. There was a schoolyard just over our back fence with a football field and a baseball field, and another one ten minutes away by bicycle. We would leave the house and be gone all day. It was an escape from the madness at home.

When things would get really bad with dad, mom would send Keith and me to stay with family or friends. We were sometimes away from home for weeks at a time. I always wonder how much the kids at school really knew about what was going on in my family life. I am sure they had no idea, but there was always an uneasiness about people finding out the truth.

One of the Boys

Athletics came naturally to me, giving me focus and purpose. It was a big part of my family's life. As you can imagine, growing up with seven brothers, I had to play sports to fit in. Playing kickball in the schoolyard with the boys, I was always one of the first to get picked. That was such a great feeling as a girl. All the turmoil at home was a blur when I was playing sports. We spent a good part of the summer at the baseball field. There was no need for actual bases, as the dirt patches around the bases were worn down to the clay.

We lived in a neighborhood with a lot of kids, but with

ten, my family had the corner on the market. I just wanted to fit in and to be accepted as "one of the guys." I would fight so hard to get to play with the guys. Perhaps this is where my desire to fight and win was ignited. I spent hundreds of hours WATCHING from the sidelines....seemed like years waiting to get the nod.

Eventually, my day to play baseball with the guys finally came. Every time I would get up to bat, Mike at short-stop would say, "Everybody move in. Kelly's up!" Oh, it would make me so mad! I wanted to hit that ball so hard. But EVERY TIME, I would swing as hard as I could, and IF I hit it at all, it would go right to—you guessed it—Mike. I just wanted to rocket one straight over his head, to show him. The day I finally did, all was good with the world.

It was a battle being so young and being a girl, which helped to form who I am today. I learned to play golf at age 7, and played softball and volleyball growing up, but basketball was my passion. It was actually my "happy place" to get away from all the strife growing up in my home. My happiest moments were on the basketball court and the driveway (where Keith and I had some of our hardest-fought battles). Sleet or snow wouldn't stop me from shooting.

A Leader At School

I always loved a good challenge, like the time I got to play on the eighth- grade basketball team as a sixth-grader. My Uncle Ed was the coach. He was so awesome as he encouraged me to play as hard as I could, no matter what the other kids thought. You know how it can be when a younger kid takes away playing time from older kids. He helped me to fight right through the challenge. All the way through high school, I stayed a step ahead. As a freshman I played varsity volleyball and basketball. I played Junior Varsity softball my freshman year, then moved up to varsity after that. We won league championships in all sports through my high school years. I was a team leader on the court all the way through high school.

Recently, I was looking back at my high school yearbook. There were so many comments about what an impact I had made in peoples' lives. It was really pretty remarkable. I was also the recipient of the Phi Beta Kappa award. I remember being quite shocked. First of all, I didn't know it existed, and I certainly didn't know what it meant. I just read the description. It recognized me for far more than being an athlete, but being a well-rounded student and a person of good character. It was quite an honor.

Reflecting on this has been important to me. As we get older and "life happens" to us, we forget what was good about our past and tend to only remember the negative. It is human nature.

Leadership was a big part of who I was becoming. I served on the student council in grade school and was the Student Council President in eighth- grade. In high school I served as class representative until my senior year, when I was the Student Council Treasurer for Regina High School. After high school, I kept exercising my leadership skills on the basketball court.

Off To College

I really wanted to play Division I basketball. I was accepted to Miami University of Ohio and was enrolled to start in the fall. My friend, Pam was going there on a scholarship, while I was going to "walk on." We were planning to be roommates. We had been playing all summer together in open gyms and working out to get ready to go. I had had chronic tendinitis in my knees for a couple of years at this point. As I thought about what it was going to take to prove myself as a walk-on, going in with knee trouble wasn't going to help my cause.

The women's basketball coach from Case Western Reserve University had been hanging out at our open gym sessions throughout the summer. She liked my game and asked me about playing at Case. My plan was to go to medical school because I wanted to do something to help people, and at that point, the most logical answer was to be a doctor. As it turned out, even though Case Western Reserve University is a Division III school, it is one of the top medical schools in the country, so it made sense for me to consider it.

Two weeks before school started, I switched to Case Western. I just loved basketball and wanted to play. I knew I would get the opportunity there, plus I would get a great education in my chosen path. So, it was a win-win.

I started out in the Pre-Med track. I loved a challenge and wanted the best, of course. I figured it would be a breeze. In high school, I finished third in my class without having to study much. Surely, college would be the same.

Surely.

As an athlete, competition on the court was a given—that's what people like me love about sports. Little did I know that the competition in academics was just as fierce. In my sophomore year, I ran into the buzz saw called Organic Chemistry. I would be studying with these silly models and didn't know a boat from a chair from an elephant standing next to me (a little O-Chem humor...OK, never mind). Needless to say, I didn't even open my box of models for the final and bombed the O-Chem final. The rubber finally met the road.

I spent the next several weeks in deep soul searching as I slammed into the realization of the difficulty of the path I had chosen. I thought back to the summer before, when I spent eight weeks at the Future Stars International basketball camp in Doylestown, PA. It was there that I found my love for coaching basketball. I wanted to share this great game with kids. That is the day, in my college dorm room, I decided that this kid playing Division III college basketball was going to be a Division I Head Coach someday. Pretty lofty dreams for a Division III kid, but nothing ever seemed impossible to me. After all, I did survive having seven older brothers.

I remember the day I called my mom to tell her the news as clear as a blue sky on a cold winter day in Ohio.

"Mom," I beamed, "I am not going to be a doctor, I am going to be a college basketball coach."

Crickets.

You can imagine my mom's deep disappointment. Being a doctor was prestigious. My older brother Steve was a doctor and she loved to brag to her friends about her son the doctor (of course, there was plenty of bragging to be heard years later, when my games were broadcast on TV).

From that day forward, I did everything I could to make that dream a reality. I spoke my goal and got specific about it. As my coach, Dani Johnson often says, "Nothing becomes dynamic until it becomes specific."

2

My Coaching Journey

IF YOU'RE AN ASPIRING COACH, please know that the work begins before you even get the interview. In fact, someone once told me, you are in an interview every day of your life. Every interaction you have has significance. You may have heard the expression "it's not what you know, it's who you know." In coaching, this is the absolute truth. It is all about building relationships. I learned this very early on and it served me well.

I am a very social person; I have always loved people and loved to have fun. I really had no fear of talking to people growing up and this carried throughout my life. I was especially comfortable speaking with adults. I liked to make people laugh and that helped make people comfortable around me. It even works with my kids' friends, but my girls aren't always so excited about my antics. But the beauty of being confident in who I am now is that I really don't worry about what others think of me. I have One to answer to.

During my playing career at Case Western Reserve, my understanding of the importance of building relationships and my confidence in speaking with adults were huge assets to me. We played in the University Athletic Association (UAA). We flew to cities like Chicago, Rochester, Atlanta, New York, and St. Louis. The men and women would play doubleheaders, with the women playing first. During the men's games, the home team would host socials for the teams to intermingle. I used this as an opportunity to introduce myself to the coaches. This is Networking 101. Over the next four years I developed some good relationships with these coaches off the court, and a reputation as a fierce competitor on the court.

With a clear goal to be a Division I Head Coach and my passion for basketball, I set out to take every opportunity that would lead to that goal. My roommate, Jeanne, was from Baltimore. She grew up going to Future Stars Camps led by Hall of Famer Cathy Rush. She was going to work at their camp that summer, so I decided to tag along. I had a blast. I ended up working there eight weeks a summer for the next few years.

The counselors were all basketball junkies. We would get up early with the campers to start the day. We worked our tails off coaching, running station work, and reffing. The best part was rushing to have a quick meal and playing the counselor games. Three times a day we would run until the directors kicked us out of the gym. I got the opportunity to work and play with some great players from big programs: I roomed with Rebecca Lobo, played with Dawn Staley (although she wouldn't remember that, I do), and many other greats from that time. It was the best job ever! We got paid peanuts, but that's beside the point. The relationships and connections I built through that experience were priceless.

Most of the girls that worked the camp played Division I basketball. In the staff games I held my own. I would get on hot shooting streaks. I was in the zone, just having a blast playing the game I loved to play. A confidence boost came when Felicia Jack, at that time an assistant at Boston College, started inquiring about who I was and what school I went to…they needed a shooter. That was a fleeting conversation, but the seed of confidence that I could fit in at the DI level was planted.

Future Stars International was a recruiting camp. These were really big before AAU became what it is today. I would be running on the sidelines officiating with Geno Auriemma, Debbie Ryan, Doug Bruno, Muffet McGraw, and many other basketball legends looking on to recruit these kids. I think I even remember Geno and Muffet sitting next to each other chatting – that was way before the "competitive heat" entered their relationship. (I have pictures….just kidding). I was sure to ham it up a bit, because I was having a blast. There wasn't a person I wouldn't talk to. I was fearless and had a dream to achieve.

My most cherished connection was getting to know Stephanie Osburn (Now Steph Norman, the awesome Associate Head Coach at Louisville). "Steph-O" we called her. Steph was the Assistant Coach at The University of Hawaii at the time. We became buds and I shared with her my dream of coaching Division I college basketball. We kept in touch as she moved around, finally settling at the University of Oregon as an assistant. One day, she called me to let me know their Graduate Assistant position had opened up, so I jumped right on it and applied. I didn't get the job. It was the summer of 1993, right after I graduated from Case. But, that didn't stop me.

Here's where all that networking pays off. Several of the counselors that I worked and became friends with also had the goal of getting into coaching, and we started going to the NCAA Final Four Tournament in an effort to do more networking with coaches. Most college coaches say they go to the Final Four to attend meetings or the coaches' development programs (and maybe they do), but the bigger truth is that it was one big party. The best place to run into coaches was in the lobby bar. As you will learn later that was a very comfortable place for me to hang out.

Southwestern University

At these events my college basketball coach, Carol Dugan, would introduce me to other coaches. One of them was Ronda Seagraves. She had been the Head Women's Basketball Coach at Allegheny College for several years. I played against them in the NCAC. After having great success there, she took the Head Coaching position at Southwestern University in Georgetown, Texas and needed an Assistant Coach. So, in June of 1993, mom and I loaded up all my belongings in a truck and drove down to Texas to start my college coaching career as the Assistant Basketball Coach and Assistant Volleyball Coach at Southwestern University.

So now, I want to share one word of wisdom I gained at that time. Never sign a lease on an apartment unseen. I am a planner. I don't remember how I got the information in those days without the internet. I found an apartment and asked Ronda to go up and take a look at the it and let me know if it was suitable. Ronda gave it a thumbs up so I made the arrangements and scheduled the moving truck to drop off my things as mom and I made the drive to Georgetown.

Two days later, we made it to the apartment. When we arrived several of the other tenants were hanging out on their front patios. It wasn't exactly what I was used to, but it would be fine. That was the feeling I had until the landlord walked us in to show us the place. We opened the kitchen cabinets and out walked a friendly little cockroach. The little fella was certainly not who I expected to be my first guest. I was in a real jam; I had already signed the lease.

Mom and I went to get cleaning supplies, but that just wasn't enough to give me peace of mind. Neither of us slept a wink that night. The next morning, I called the landlord and told him this is not what I signed up for. I needed to find another place to live. I went out that day and found a nice, new, clean apartment complex and negotiated out of the lease with the landlord. All was made right. I called Ronda and asked her what the heck she was thinking when she gave the thumbs up. It turns out she never even went inside. She said she saw a baby outside with the families hanging on the porch. If it was good enough for a baby it must be OK. Lesson learned: things aren't always what they appear to be.

But none of that took away my excitement to get started in my new position. A full-time Division III Assistant Coach position was an excellent opportunity for me. I was the only assistant to both programs. I had a lot of responsibility and wore a lot of hats, including recruiting, coaching, travel, individual workouts. You name it, I did it.

Perhaps the biggest task was organizing and managing the recruiting for both programs. I spent a lot of time working the phones. This was a great experience to prepare me to take on my next role, plus there wasn't a whole lot of pressure. Division III recruiting is a numbers game: develop as many relationships as you can with talented players on your list and the Law of Averages will do its thing. Since there is no athletic scholarship money, the decision is heavily weighted on the financial packages the athlete is offered. Your best bet in closing the deal was to find the strong academic kids who would qualify for a lot of academic scholarships.

University of Oregon

I was honored to have my first real coaching role and I wasn't in any hurry to leave Southwestern, but that burning to get to the Division I level wouldn't subside. So when Stephanie Osburn called me from her new position at the University of Oregon to tell me the Graduate Assistant had moved on, and the job was open again, I was bound and determined to get that job. It didn't bother me that she left because the working environment wasn't the best. There were only 300 Division I schools at the time. I would do whatever I had to do to break into the Division I coaching circle.

The Women's Basketball Head Coach at that time was Jody Runge, and Stephanie let me know up front that she was a tough one. Steph really wanted me to get the job but she really had no influence on the decision. I would have to do my homework to get in front of her. So I did. I called the University of Oregon MBA office to find out what it would take for me to get accepted to the graduate program before I had even talked with her.

The AAU Nationals, where EVERY coach in the country would attend to recruit, was in Cleveland, Ohio, my hometown. I arranged my summer vacation to go to Cleveland. I mapped out the schedule of where the west coast teams were playing, figuring Jody would have to come through and watch them at some point. I camped out in the various gyms, waiting for her arrival.

When I found her, she was sitting against the bleachers in the main gym at Cleveland State. I boldly walked up to her and introduced myself: "Hi, Coach Runge. My name is Kelly Kebe. I am going to be your Graduate Assistant."

"Oh, really?" she replied, a little incredulous (I suppose I would have been, too).

I proceeded to explain to her that I had researched the MBA program and was already accepted. All she had to do was say yes. We sat and talked for a bit. I had no idea what she was thinking when I left the gym, but I gave it all I had.

My gamble paid off. Two weeks later, I got the call and began the move from Texas to Oregon.

The University of Oregon was awesome. I was in the PAC-10, baby! (Nope, that is not a typo)

In only my second real coaching position, I had broken into the Division I coaching circle—not an easy thing to do in the 1990s, when there were only two full-time assistants and a graduate assistant. As a Graduate Assistant at that time, you worked your tail off, went to grad school full-time and got a stipend of $345 a month. It was an incredible challenge and an amazing learning experience. We practiced from 7:00 a.m. to 10:00 a.m. every morning, then I was off to class starting at 11:00 a.m. Most nights, I would be up studying until 1:00 or 2:00 a.m. In 1995 the GA position was bumped up to be called the "Restricted Earnings" Coach. Earnings were restricted all right. But getting a check for $12,000 for the year was amazing!

In the MBA program I was in classes with people with five to ten years of corporate experience. I was in a bit over my head, but I learned to find the people who were willing to help me succeed. Juan became one of my great allies. He would make my head spin by the way he could whip around the computer and create the spreadsheets for the business class assignments. Any time there was group work I would buddy up with Juan. He was brilliant at Excel spreadsheets and I was great at presenting. We made a great team!

I also learned how to ask the right questions in class. I learned that I wasn't the only one that had the question, but I had the courage to ask. It was a matter of time management for me. I didn't have the time to spend looking up the answers, so I preferred to get them from the instructors. It was a grind, but I loved every minute of it.

Learning to Work Smart

Working for Jody Runge was not all rainbows and unicorns, that's for sure. She was tough and demanding. I was in charge of team travel. Fortunately, I liked working out the logistics. I didn't know how much pull Jody thought I had until we were in the airport waiting on a flight that got delayed hour after hour. Our incoming plane was having mechanical issues and hadn't left the previous airport, and was obviously NOT at the gate, so we had some time to kill. I was just walking around the terminal when Jody tracked me down. She pulled me aside and growled, "Do something about this!" Wow! I was honored that she thought I could work magic in the airport. What was I supposed to do? Find a new plane out of thin air? She could be unrealistic at times, but then, what Head Coach isn't?

I had the opportunity to do a lot of great things at Oregon. I learned a lot as a Graduate Assistant and I was so excited to be on the coaching staff. Steph was a recruiting machine and had a true passion for this most important aspect of the job. She would pump out mailer after mailer to the kids, while I helped her to create motivational pieces and materials to keep Oregon on the forefront of their minds. She was awesome at including me in the process and "showing me the ropes." She was really good at recruiting. You need to have good players to win. I was able to take those valuable recruiting skills with me and utilize them in my future roles.

One responsibility I really enjoyed was working with the Duck Club. We had amazing fans that were very zealous about the program, and I had the responsibility of setting up post-game socials and growing the club. I put into practice the marketing skills that I had been learning in the MBA program to help with this project. After all the home games,

Jody would come over and meet with the group and share highlights of the game.

Coach Litz (Fred Litzenberger) was another great mentor. He was a defensive guru and a total basketball technician. I would sit with him for hours and talk hoops, learning to master the defensive game. This is where I learned the mastery of the "close- out." If you know Coach Litz—and many in the game do—you can hear him shouting, "throw your hands back, chop your feet." It was a joy to work with him. He was the master of the scouting reports as well. He was very detail- oriented in his presentation. He emphasized defending the opponent to keep their best players from beating us. I definitely took that skill with me, too.

But, my favorite person from that season of my life was Carol Jaeger, the equipment manager. Her office was in the basement of MAC Court. It was the loudest and most "rickety" office in the world...that's no joke. You could hear every footstep on the court, every ball bouncing like the erratic beat of a tribal battle cry. I'm not sure how she stayed sane. I would park at MAC Court to go to class every day, and most days I popped in to say hello to Carol. She was my mom away from home. As you know, coaches can be a little obsessive about things, and sometimes my position was stressful. I would chat with Carol and she would listen and share insights about the staff; she had been there forever and had seen and heard it all. Overall, it was an incredible experience. I finished my stint as a Graduate Assistant at Oregon with back-to-back trips to the NCAA Tournament under my belt.

Texas Christian University

In April 1996, I was just about to finish my MBA at the University of Oregon when Mike Petersen, who had just taken the Head Coaching job at Texas Christian University

(TCU), called Barb Walker, the Senior Women's Administrator at the University of Oregon, to ask if she had any recommendations on coaches. Barb oversaw the women's basketball program at Oregon, and I had many opportunities to work with her in the NCAA planning for our program. This gave me the opportunity to work one-on-one with her. She knew my work ethic and my desire to expand my basketball coaching resume (not to mention that the working environment was not exactly roses and sunshine). Barb was awesome, and I am still grateful that she told Mike about me. As always, it really is who you know that gets you in the door for interviews.

The next week, I was flying to Fort Worth to interview with Coach Petersen for one of the assistant positions. I remember him showing me around the campus and standing on the track with the warm sunshine beating down on us. I felt right at home with the Texas sun. I had missed it. The interview went well and Mike offered me the job. Soon, I was moving back to Texas, going from being a Duck to a Horned Frog.

TCU presented me with a fantastic challenge. We were on a mission, because, by all measures, TCU had one of the worst programs in college basketball at that time. We were competing in the Western Athletic Conference (WAC), which was the biggest conference in the US, with 16 teams spanning from Tulsa, Oklahoma to Hawaii.

We had a lot of work to do.

The first thing was to change the mentality of the athletes from losing to winning. We were there to win, but it takes time and patience to change the culture. There was a lack of discipline and work ethic and not a ton of talent, but the cupboard wasn't totally bare. We had to go to work on the recruiting front.

The great thing about Texas—especially the Dallas/Fort

Worth area—is that there is always a ton of talent there. We wouldn't have to go far to recruit, but we had to change the perception of the program. I learned a lot working with the staff there, and we had a blast working hard to fix the program. Mike, Art and I were like the Three Musketeers, attending pretty much every recruiting event together. We hit Texas hard. By the end of the summer we were simply "babysitting" the Sutton twins out of Gunter, and Tracy Gahan from McKinney. They played on Team Texas, the same AAU team.

The twins had slightly different skill sets: Amy was a point guard and Jill a shooting guard. The problem was that they wanted to play together, but there weren't many schools willing to sign both of them. That was to our advantage. Tracy was at a slightly different level, she was a 6'1" shooter being stalked by Iowa State, among other Big XII schools. She was a long shot, but we hung in with her, too. Signing the Sutton twins was a huge get for TCU, and they worked very well in Coach Pete's system.

As an Assistant Coach, you spend a ton of time on the road. For a young single, this is a great way to run around the country and meet people. I enjoyed the recruiting trail. We would recruit against a lot of the same schools and see the same coaches in the gyms. Friendships and camaraderie develop, even though we were competing for players. The mid-major Texas schools (TCU, North Texas, and SMU) were all chasing the same bunch of kids. There were a bunch of assistants who still loved to play, so we would find a gym somewhere and get a pick-up game together. That's what happens when you have a bunch of basketball junkies needing to get a workout in. We would get a late game in and then grab dinner, only to get up and do it all over again the next day. Recruiting was a lot like the movie "Groundhog Day," starring Bill Murray.

Once you established your "short list" of players, you would just "sit" on kids. We spent countless hours traveling to one tournament after another, just to watch the same kids play over and over again, with the same coaches sitting in the stands. It really is a bit ridiculous when you think about it, but that's what we did. You couldn't let yourself be "outdone" by another program. This is where the coaching relationships can develop.

I became really good friends with Katie Abrahamson, then an Assistant at Iowa State (Now the Head Coach at Central Florida). Katie and I were charged with following Tracy Gahan all over the country. Iowa State was a top 15 program at the time and TCU was in a building stage. Tracy was from McKinney, TX but had some family roots in Iowa. So, we hung in there, hoping we still had a chance to snag a top recruit. Katie and I would go from gym to gym watching Tracy. In the end, Iowa State won that one. Little did I know that I'd get to coach Tracy anyway.

Iowa State had just lost an Assistant Coach to a Head Coaching position. Head Coach Bill Fennelly called TCU to ask permission to talk to me about the coaching position. Although I loved TCU and the staff, it was a great move for me on my quest to become a Division I Head Coach. I was moving to Ames, Iowa. Ironically, two months after I left TCU, Mike Petersen left TCU to move over to the men's side of the game as an assistant at the University of Minnesota. If I had not taken that position at Iowa State, I would have been out of a job searching for a place to land. Someone was looking out for me.

Iowa State

My time at Iowa State was a dream come true. In my first month on staff we spent two weeks traveling across the

Netherlands, Norway, Sweden, and Denmark with the team. From there, I hit the recruiting trails with Bill and Katie. We had a great time. I knew how to do this. It was all the same game, just wearing a different uniform and getting to chase better talent. It was an honor to wear the Cyclone gear and represent a great program.

In recruiting we were now competing against the top schools in the country for talent. This meant that the coaches that I would be getting bleacher butt with when recruiting were the likes of Pat Summit and Andy Landers and Jody Conradt, and Gary Blair, and , and , and...Vic Shaffer, who was only an assistant back then as well. Jeff Walz was an assistant at Nebraska when Iowa State would dominate that rivalry, he must have learned so much coaching against Iowa State to take him to his success today. (That's a little humor for coaches who know the game). There are so many that are still strong in the game who I had the chance to coach against or get to know on the recruiting trails.

The most memorable experiences were game days at Hilton Coliseum. Each game was incredible. At that time, we were the third-ranked team in the country in attendance behind Tennessee and Connecticut. Imagine playing in front of 11,000 fans every home game.

Iowa State had a "Little Clone" club for kids, with first-come-first-served seating in the end zone by our bench. I would make a point to be on the court an hour before tip-off. that's when the doors would open and the kids would flood the stands like water rushing over a waterfall. It was a thunderous roar as the bleachers shook and parents and kids poured into the seats. Then the game would start. What an awesome feeling to hear the crowd roar as we poured in record-breaking three pointers.

We played an up-tempo game that was led by the match-up zone we played. Our defense created our offense, allowing us to get out and shoot threes at a rapid pace. I learned a lot from Coach Fennelly in those three years about different zones, junk defenses, and how to be creative on the defensive end to wreak havoc on the opponent.

In game prep, I would spend hours and hours watching game film, mastering the tendencies of the opponents' players, creating the scouting report to take away the strengths of their team. Our zone and junk defenses were extremely effective ways to shut down their best players and hide some personnel deficiencies we had. One of the greatest moments I remember is beating Oklahoma in the Big XII Tournament. We had to find a way to stop Stacey Dales. Man, she was tough. But, we put all our efforts into stopping her. If we could stop Dales, we would win the Big XII Tournament Championship. It was a great effort by the players and an awesome victory for the program.

It was such an honor to work with Bill Fennelly. At that time he was so highly regarded as one of the greats in women's college basketball. He is still to this day as he has just celebrated 25 years as the head coach at Iowa State. His honor and respect of others is what has kept him at the helm for so long. We had great success at Iowa State over my three seasons as an assistant. In 2000, we were Big XII Conference and Tournament Champions; in 2001, we were Big XII Tournament Champions, and in both 2000 and 2001 we made it to the NCAA Sweet 16. To date, that has been the greatest stretch in Iowa State women's basketball history and I was so fortunate to be a part of that success.

It would be terribly short-sighted of me to neglect the fact that Iowa was where I met the man who would become my best friend and life companion, my husband, Todd. To date, he is the biggest and BEST recruit I ever signed, no coincidence that he is 6'8". (I have to give credit to Bill Fennelly for that line. He always referred to his wife, Deb, that way).

Meeting Todd was a big win for me among so many, and capped off an amazing run that launched me into a new chapter of my life.

Dreams Fulfilled: University of Akron

It was April of 2002 when I got the call from Mike Thomas, the Athletic Director at the University of Akron. The words rang through my whole soul: "Would you like to be the Head Coach of the Akron Zips?"

I was ecstatic and eager to take on my new role. I had big goals for this program. I had come from some great basketball success as well as experience turning around a program. All that paired with my vast experience in every aspect of running a Division I program, I was hungry, eager, energetic, and ready to take on the world.

In the midst of this, Todd and I were planning to get married in Cleveland. The plan was for me to head to Akron and get things started. I lived in an Extended Stay Hotel while Todd wrapped up his job in Iowa.

The first task was to get there and meet the team. What a bunch it was!

The most obvious issue was the lack of success of the program. At that time the RPI was (if I remember correctly) 296 out of 300. That means only 4 teams in the country had a worse RPI. I should have arranged to play those teams 4 times each in the pre-season (ha ha – basketball scheduling humor). I felt confident we could turn things around. We did it at TCU.

To win games you need talent, I learned that there were a few players on scholarship that had transferred from Division III schools, but I had to honor all the scholarships that were given. In other words, I couldn't just "clean house" and start all over. I am also a person of principle. Don't misunderstand,

I am not saying I am perfect. But, I had been groomed by my mentors in a good way to be honorable and do the right thing when it came to the players.

The next task was to hire a staff. I had some people in mind that I thought would be good to work with and I wanted people that I knew and trusted— people I had history with, friends in the business.

Here's a quick word of wisdom to my fellow coaches: it may not always be good to hire "friends." It makes it more difficult to make changes in your staff when necessary. The loyalty of a friendship can get in the way of making good decisions when needed.

So, the staff was set and we were off and running. We had a lot of work to do to turn around the fourth-worst RPI team in the country. The first year was great as we worked well together. The athletes were excited for a change and (for the most part) began to conform to what was expected of a Division I athlete.

The key words are "for the most part."

There were other distractions in the program that I had not had experience dealing with my past, such as kids smoking marijuana. This was a whole new wrinkle to anything I had faced. That was a big distraction early on and challenged us as a staff. It was not an easy fix that's for sure.

We worked really hard to change the culture of the program. We brought discipline and structure to the program and the desire to work together and compete hard every single day.

The first year was under our belts with little improvement in the win column. We just didn't have the horses to finish games out and win. There was improvement, but it was a far cry from where we wanted to be. But then we brought in a solid recruiting class with more athleticism and length, which resulted in a bit more success on the court, but competing in a tough mid-major conference, the Mid- American Conference (MAC), made it very challenging.

I was focused on the X's and O's; I really believed it was all the on-court work that would lead to our success. I would spend hours and hours poring over film, prepping for each opponent. If I knew the opponent inside and out, we could work out ways to win. The harder you work the better you get, right? I believed I could out-work and out-prep any coach in the conference. I believed we could beat every opponent we stepped out to face. I believed that, if I just instilled that belief in all our players through showing them we were the best-prepared team and knew every move they would make, we would win.

It doesn't work that way.

You see, other coaches prepare well, too. Curt Miller at Bowling Green was a great coach when it came to being well-prepared; the difference was that he had a bit more talent around him. They were the top of the MAC at the time. Kent State was still tough under Bob Lindsay, and the rest of the MAC was no picnic. There were so many great coaches, including Suzy Merchant, Mark Ehlen, Maria Fantanarosa, Carol Owens all of whom had very solid programs and knew how to prepare teams well. Every night was a battle. The kids played and competed so hard in every game. We kept the games close, but just came up short, losing many by single digits. Call them "moral victories" if you want, but unfortunately, that doesn't cut it.

The Beginning of the End

This is probably about the time that some words that were spoken about me in my past began to take root.... I heard that it was said by a former colleague that "she's not good enough to be coaching at this level". I'm sure it wasn't a big deal to the person who said it, and I should have blown it off and forgotten about it.

But it planted a seed.

That comment lingered under the soil of my mind, silently burrowing tiny roots of doubt and taking hold, alongside the seeds of my parents' unhealthy marriage feeding my need to fit in and feel accomplished.

When things were going well it was easy to brush it aside. However, in those quiet moments it would float back into my thoughts, always there, waiting for an opportunity to sprout.

The point here is that words are seed. Whether spoken directly or second-hand. Once spoken they are out there for the receiver to take or leave. It really doesn't matter who said the words, but that they were spoken for the hearer to take or leave.

The second season had some improvements. We remained positive as we had some new recruits that were going to help us turn this thing around. Unfortunately, they were freshman and couldn't bear the whole load. The season improved a bit but not nearly at the rate that I had hoped or planned.

As my third season at Akron was getting underway, I was due with my first child. I had it all planned out with my doctor: our child would be born on November 10, which would give me about two weeks to get back on my feet so that I could go to the Bahamas to play in a tournament—with my new baby in tow.

Did you read what I just wrote?

In case you missed it, this was the first real sign that I wasn't entirely in control. Molly Marie Kennedy was born on November 18th at 12:01 am. I had no idea at the time what had just happened, but it turned our lives upside-down. I was so obsessed with MY career and MY team, that we left the hospital just 35 hours after I gave birth, because I "needed" to listen to our home opener and I couldn't get good radio reception in the hospital. As we drove past the University of Akron exit on the way home from the hospital, Todd looked at me and said, "don't even think about it."

I totally thought I was doing the right thing. I was committed to this team. I was the leader. No one could do what I would do. In reality, I felt I needed to have control, and I was afraid to give that leadership up to someone else, so I hadn't prepared the team or my staff for my absence. I had never had a baby before, so I had no idea what I was getting into. My perspective was so messed up. I would certainly make different choices today.

It is so important to put together a staff that works well together. Being a great leader means understanding your people and getting them on the same page. This was new ground for me. I did "staff retreats," but they just didn't have the effect I was looking for. I followed a lot in the footsteps of my mentors. Experience was my classroom. Some of my past staff experiences were good and some were not so good, but I used it all the best I knew how at the time.

Now that I was a Head Coach, I wasn't in the teachable mode. After all, as a Head Coach, I was supposed to have the answers.

By the fourth year, things were not running smoothly. I couldn't look at things objectively and make the changes that needed to be made. Loyalty was a big thing to me, but my loyalty to friends in my coaching crew was starting to hurt me. Things were not going well and I could feel it. My own self-control was diminishing as the pressure to win and get things back on track mounted. The University hired a new Athletic Director, and it pressed upon me a greater urgency to win more games.

During quiet moments, the negative words spoken about me would creep back into my head: "she's not good enough to be here." It tore at my heart, but it made sense. We weren't performing at the level we needed to because I wasn't good enough. What do you do when you feel inadequate? You push harder: work harder, prepare more, watch more film, practice more, put in new plays, change things up on the court--that was surely the answer. It became a vicious cycle.

Suddenly, another season was over and we had come up short again. The air in the office was as thick as West Virginia mountain fog. After another tumultuous day where my gut felt like it was ready to explode, I bolted up from my desk and left the office. That day, I had my sweet little Molly with me; she was my only source of peace. The cold rain outside matched the prickly gloom inside my heart. Molly cooed as I slipped her into her car seat, but I was too far gone to appreciate it. I slumped behind the wheel and turned the key. As the engine roared to life, I felt a sob rise up from my guts. I gasped to keep it in, but it was too late. I didn't want my innocent baby girl to hear it, so I quickly cranked up the radio to hide my grieving from her.

Carrie Underwood's hit song, "Jesus Take The Wheel" thundered through the speakers as wave after wave of sorrow, anger, disappointment, and fear heaved up through my chest. I couldn't hold it back. Every cell of my body wanted to scream to relieve the pressure. I had to keep my voice down and my eyes on the road, but I had never wanted so badly to turn the car off the next exit and disappear.

Each wave of emotion pushed a prayer to my lips: help me, guide me, fix this mess. I didn't know what I wanted anymore, and I certainly didn't know how to pray about it, but these whispers were all I had. They were all I needed.

It All Comes Crashing Down

A week later, I had my review with the new Athletic Director. I had met him before, but in four months' time, we had only spoken one other time, and I didn't have any kind of relationship with him. The Senior Women's Administrator (SWA) was in the office as well, which probably should have been a red flag to me, but I missed it. I walked in and sat down, anticipating some mostly-positive constructive criticism. I certainly wasn't expecting an enthusiastic "atta-girl" pat on the back. We weren't performing at the level I wanted and I knew it. However, I had one year left on my contract so I really thought I was "safe". I didn't see anything that was coming.

He started with a cordial hello, please sit down, and all the normal pleasantries, but all I remember him saying is, "We are asking you to resign or be fired; it is your choice."

The words hung in space.

My choice.

What the heck does that mean?

There was no warning, it was a complete blindside. I didn't even know how to respond. I was absolutely devastated. Speechless.

The days that followed were filled with anger and bitterness. I got word that there had been meetings with some of my staff before this all shook out. My thoughts were swirling like a tornado in my brain. What did they say? They must have had something to do with this. I knew that things weren't great with my staff—clearly that was the only explanation. I had been sabotaged.

I understand if you are thinking, "man, you are a crazy woman." At that point in time, it's safe to say that I *was* going a bit crazy. It was a traumatic experience. "Surely," I thought, "someone else has to pay for my pain." If they had anything to do with getting me fired, they would have to pay the price with me. I know this sounds horrible, but this is the truth and I told you I would be completely honest with you. Someday, someone is going to call me as a reference for one of these ungrateful saboteurs and I will make sure they don't get that opportunity. Well, by the grace of God, nobody called. In all reality, why would they call and ask my opinions, anyway? My point in sharing this is that when we harbor bitterness and anger, it does horrible things to us internally and externally. It can cause us to do things or say things which are totally out of character.

There were a few phone calls from supportive friends in those early days. This is such an awkward thing. Do you call? Do you not call? You really don't know until it happens to you. You feel embarrassed and shameful, like you're alone on a deserted island. You think no one wants to talk to you. In fact it was my own pride and ego that created those feelings of isolation. Now, when I hear about people so flippantly talking about firing coaches, I really feel for the coaches. It's so easy to say, "fire the guy" until you realize that he is a human being with a family, who poured his heart and soul into that job, whether you think he did it well or not.

I had heard coaches joking around, saying, "either you have been fired or you will be some day, it's just a matter of how long you've been in the business." I never thought it would happen to me. I guess nobody ever does.

I was in a terrible state of mind. Up to that moment, I was a college basketball coach—that was who I was. It was my identity as a person, and that had just been stripped from me. The shame and embarrassment stuck with me for many years. It was hidden beneath my excuses of, "I don't want to coach anymore, it's the best thing for my family," or "I am staying in the game doing other things," as I worked my business helping athletes with recruiting. I had so much doubt in myself: "I guess I wasn't good enough anyway," I would recite to myself. So, I did other things that did not involve coaching for a long time.

The Year Off

I had a year left on my contract, so I got a severance package, contingent on my not coaching anywhere else, which allowed me to sit out and figure things out. Todd, who had been doing the "Mr. Mom" thing, went back to working full-time and I stayed home. It was nice for a while. I began to see life on the other side of the basketball lines. We had time to take vacations and do things a "normal" family would do. I was ambitious and driven, as most coaches are, and started business after business. Our family continued to grow with Finley being born in 2007 and Caitlin late in 2008, just 18 months apart. We had a house full of toddlers to keep us very busy. In addition to the kids, I would keep myself busy chasing the next best idea. I had plenty to do, but no matter what I never felt fulfilled.

The conflict of my "stolen identity" ever lingered in my mind. It was a very painful process. There were many tears in this conflict, but without conflict there can be no growth. It reminds me of the old expression that says, "that which does not kill me makes me stronger." God says it more eloquently in I John 5:10: "And the God of all grace, who called you to his eternal glory in Christ, after you have suffered a little while, will himself restore you and make you strong, firm and steadfast."

I began to gain some clarity in my life to look at the good fruit in my life. It took years of peeling back layer and layer of negativity that had rooted in my thoughts, but the unveiling has been so worthwhile. Of course, I am human and will continue to mess up, so I have to train myself to look at the fruit and identify it for what it is. The good stays and bad has to be plucked away. It is a constant process that I need to go through.

I have shared all this with you because we are all broken in some way. We all have scars and wounds that keep us from being that amazing person God created us to be—the one loved and favored by God Himself. My hope is that my story would help to heal you and give you a more fulfilled life.

I hear you say to yourself, "how can I be favored? What I did was way worse than what you did. I have messed up so many times. How can I set things right?" I am here to tell you that the TRUTH shall make you free. God already knows all about you and what you did. God is love, and "Love is patient, love is kind ... it is not self-seeking, it is not easily angered, it keeps no record of wrongs." (1 Corinthians 13:4-5). He does not keep score! You did what you did. He already knows it. He just wants you to come to Him in love and know that you are forgiven. By the blood of Jesus you are set free and forgiven.

That is TRUTH.

In John 14:6, Jesus told His disciples, "I am the way and the truth and the life. No one comes to the Father except through me."

What I have found in my dealings with people is that, if God is in your life, there is greater fulfillment in all that you do. His goodness is shown in what you DO, because you put God first. He has defined who you are, and all you do is a reflection of God, therefore it is good—win, lose, or tie.

3
Post-Coaching Realities

I STILL CARRIED around hidden bitterness and shame from losing my coaching job (the core of my identity). I stayed away from the newspaper and what was going on at Akron. I had scheduled for success that final year and the new coach was taking "my players" and a lighter schedule and doing what I was supposed to have the opportunity to do – win more games. Although that was salt in the wound, I did not sit around idly and wallow in my sorrows. I am a doer and doers do. Over the next eight years I started several businesses. My sweet husband, bless his heart, supported me in every single venture. I mean, I could paint a positive picture on any business idea, and he knew I would work hard at it, but I'm sure he thought I was nuts sometimes.

I had a recruiting assistance business for about 6 years, which went well until I got tired of working evenings and weekends (it was very similar to the demands of coaching). Next, I got involved in a direct sales business, helping people with nutrition and hoping to help athletes with sports nutrition. This was rewarding in its own way, but I wanted to make real money. I was approached about an insurance business opportunity. This seemed like an awesome way to help businesses meet their insurance needs at a lower cost for their bottom line. I knew absolutely nothing about health insurance, but I was shown an idea that made sense, so I ran with that and got an insurance license.

While I could have let this new season of my life refine me and build a deeper character inside me, I chose to spend it chasing money. If only I could make more money, I reasoned, that would solve all my insecurity issues. If nothing else, it would give my family a more comfortable life. At least, it would allow me to build a house worthy of a Division I coach. Do you see where I'm going with this?

Finally, Some Direction

As I thrashed around from opportunity to opportunity, a friend told me about a business seminar where I could learn to make more money. I bit that bait like a barracuda: finally, the solution I was looking for! In April 2014, Todd and I went to *First Steps To Success*, which we thought was simply a business seminar. We quickly discerned that it was much more than that.

Dani Johnson began to share stories about the life of abuse, drugs, and shame she came from, and how she went from being homeless to making a million dollars in her first two years in business. As she broke down the essentials of building a business, I found myself leaning forward with my notepad, grabbing every word, waiting for the big tip that was going to make me rich.

And then she dropped this question: "how do you answer to your boss?"

You become an entrepreneur, the thinking goes, so you can "be your own boss." I certainly bought into that thinking and I don't think I'm the only one. In front of over 1,000 people, I blurted out a question of my own: "what if you don't have a boss?"

Without missing a beat, she wheeled around toward me and quietly dropped a bomb in my lap: "That's your number one problem."

I sat there in my own moment of silence, as she continued teaching around me. I couldn't even process it. What the heck does that mean? Suddenly, it dawned upon me, as she pointed to the sky. My jaw dropped and my whole being just sank into my chair. The revelation brought me to my knees: my boss was God and I had surely not been working for Him.

It wasn't that I didn't believe in God. I was a good Catholic girl: I went to church every Sunday, had our kids in Catholic schools and did all the weekly routines that come with Catholic faith. But I came to realize in a heartbeat that I did not have a relationship with my Heavenly Father. That moment began a long, slow journey of rediscovering myself, and became the catalyst for this book.

I still had this deep yearning to make money, and I was focused on listening for strategies to increase my income. I still had a powerful drive and passion to make a great contribution to our family.

After all, more money would solve everything...right?

I still had the need to replace the six-figure income I lost as a coach. But even deeper was the emptiness that I thought came from losing all that income.

Toward the end of the seminar, Dani taught on the differences between personality groups. My group is the drivers, the go-getters, always wanting to win. Competition and control are our lifeblood. I felt like she was looking right at me when she said, "you were meant for more." Yes! That's what I was looking for: more money, bigger business, the top of the ladder...right? Isn't that what she meant? That's what I heard. When she invited us to her next seminar, I jumped up and got my ticket. I knew I was on the trail to answer that yearning in my heart.

A few weeks later, I was in Atlanta, sitting in front of this same trainer, looking for the "more" she promised. The next seminar was her advanced leadership course, Creating A Dynasty, which is designed to take all of the teaching from *First Steps To Success* and go deeper, in part through face-to-face application opportunities. Certainly, I was going to hear that one tip that was going to break open the money floodgates for me. I just knew it.

Oh, she delivered the "more," that's for sure. It wasn't necessarily the "more" I was looking for, but it was precisely what my Father God knew I needed to be a healthy wife, mom, and professional. I wouldn't have asked for it, but I can't argue with the fruit: a softer heart, richer relationships, and an identity as a Daughter of the Most High God, which allows me to walk in confident humility.

In the years since, I have gone back to her events multiple times, and each time, I not only recalibrate myself with what I have learned in the past, I go deeper in working on myself. I have changed my focus from business growth to personal and spiritual growth. As God and my coach have worked with me to peel away the onion-layers of my tough exterior, I have begun to see my true identity. I was not a coach; coaching was what I did. My true identity is "child of the Most High." I'll show you what that means as we go on.

Clearing Away Boulders

I don't have any farmers in my immediate family, but there are plenty of them around Ohio and Iowa, and I have gotten to know many through coaching. I have learned from them that you can't plant seeds just anywhere; you have to prepare the soil first. First, you remove any trees and plants that will interfere with your crop. Then you dig up and remove boulders, then large rocks, then small rocks, then gravel. The soil is ready for seeds when it is soft and clear of roots and debris. Personal development and coaching follow the same basic process. Through the rest of the book, you will see me identifying and removing boulders, rocks, and gravel from different parts of my life to prepare my soul – my heart- for an orchard of success. My hope is that it will encourage you to pursue the same process in your own life.

Getting To The Roots

I find I'm having a hard time analyzing my decisions as I look back. We all go through life doing what we think is best. If you are advancing in your career and people are calling to hire you, it's easy to figure that you must be doing something right. It's hard to see clearly what you are doing wrong until someone brings it to your attention. I don't remember my Head Coaches doing year-end evaluations with me. Knowing what I know now, I would have asked more questions and asked for feedback. But that is a characteristic of humility, which to be honest, is a quality that I did not have much of at that time. I would say I possessed more fear of someone telling me that I screwed up and needed to do better—the fear of rejection.

Where did that fear come from?

Through this new process of personal development, I realized I needed to start digging down to expose the roots of my insecurities before I could move forward. My personal development coach, Dani Jonson, would say, "follow the fruit to the root." Where you see good fruit in your life (e.g., peace, confidence, wisdom, honesty, etc.), you prune it, because pruning something makes it grow and multiply. Where you see bad fruit (e.g., fear, shame, embarrassment, abandonment, etc.), you need to follow that root back to where it starts and cut it out of your heart.

Getting to the root of unhealthy thought patterns is often difficult for people, because it usually involves reliving and confronting traumatic moments from your life. Most of the destructive behaviors that show up in our lives originate from defense mechanisms (sometimes called "ego") that we build to protect ourselves from pain as children. Researchers suggest that 80% or more of your adult personality is formed before you are six years old. If you are exposed to abuse, shame, abandonment, or other traumas as a small child, your inner self will work overtime to protect you from it ever happening again. If you heard words of rejection or shame spoken over you as a child, your soul will go out of its way to build up a wall. The problem is, it creates barriers that keep others from getting close to you, and you grow up lonely, ashamed, and unhealthy. Worse yet, those shaming and rejecting words always find ways to creep through cracks in the barrier and play out through your life.

For example, if you accepted the thought, "you're not good enough" as a child, you may grow up extra-competitive, arrogant, or aggressive in an effort to prove those words wrong. But then, when a failure happens, like your team losing game after game, the "not good enough" words will creep through to the surface and shame you in your quiet moments. This is what leads people to run to other comforts to silence those whispers in their head. As I told you, drinking in my early years was my silencer. I'm not much of a drinker anymore because I have found my comfort in my God. However, the more I understand about this, the more I have compassion for people who drink, or seek other sources of comfort to silence those internal voices.

Let's look at some places my "you're not good enough" words came from:

- That kid on baseball field
- Verbally abusive father
- The coach who said, "I have forgotten more basketball than you will ever know"
- The colleague who said, "you're not good enough to coach here"

Here is what I have learned. People are going to say things and do things that are negative and degrading to you. Hurting people say hurtful things. What comes out of their mouth is sourced from the condition of their heart. It is crap that is flying at you – THEIR CRAP. You have the choice to eat it or reject it. If you eat it, it becomes toxic inside of you and creates a belief system of "not good enough." If you choose to not listen and receive it as truth, it doesn't become a part of you.

Now, if only we could get every six-year-old in the world to understand and apply this concept consistently. Good luck with that.

Turns out I had chosen to scarf down other peoples trash talk throughout my life…So, the work began to identify the rejection thoughts in my life, root them out and kill them. This is the hard work, however, getting to the goodness that is buried inside of you is well worth digging through the weeds that life's experiences have planted inside.

The fact is everyone is dealing with their pile of crap that has been heaped on them. Gross, I know, but true. You have your own to deal with. Taking on someone else's manure is a choice. Forcing yours on someone else is also a choice. If you can identify it for what it is, then you can put it where it belongs…and flush!

I Got Fired!

Getting fired from a job, any job, can be a devastating experience for anybody. In coaching, outsiders talk about coaches getting fired as water cooler chit-chat. It easily rolls off of sports fans' tongues (e.g., "Oh, just fire the guy already. He doesn't know what he is doing.") without giving a single thought to "the guy," who has a wife and kids that just uprooted his family and moved across the country to start all over. It has a greater effect on "the guy's" life than you even care to think about. And why should he be fired? Because he lost more games than he won? We're missing something here.

Don't get me wrong, I understand the fact that he is making a very good salary to do what fans seem to think is the most glamorous job, coaching college and pro sports. But, I am here to tell you it is not as glamorous as you think. It's a TON of work, with 80- and 90-hour work weeks in season, and at least 50-hour work weeks out of season, recruiting and chasing kids all over the country. There is way more to it than the 40 minutes you see them coaching at game time.

The next time you casually shout out, "fire the guy", stop for a second and think about what you are saying. Maybe stop for a second and pray for him and his family. More than likely, his family is undergoing enormous pressures you can't imagine. Getting fired could be the most devastating thing in his life. Heck, it may even take him twelve years to get over it.

That is where my truth—and hopefully an offering of healing for others who read this—comes in. It honestly took me nine years just to admit to myself and others that I didn't resign, I got fired. It then took me another three years to totally heal from the wounds that were opened on that fateful day in 2006. If you're feeling wounded from a job loss (or a complete career collapse), I hope the words I share with you will help lead you to a path of healing and self-understanding.

It was 2006 when the hammer came down on me. I was lost for a long time after that. I would mask my feelings of shame and embarrassment in my new role as a mom and business owner. I considered myself an expert in the college recruiting arena and was able to use my coaching experience to illuminate the murky processes that coaches put their recruits through; to help students and their parents navigate that transition in their lives. The most important piece was discussing with them the reality of which level they could be most successful. I really enjoyed educating the athletes and parents, as well as the enlightening conversations I could have with them, but there was always this nagging in the back of my mind, why aren't you coaching?

The answer was easy at first. I had three kids within four years. By 2008, we had our third sweet daughter, so my hands were full. I was bogged down with all that it took to stay sane as a mom of three toddlers. This was way harder than coaching to me. There was so much that was unpredictable and out of my control. It really showed me how much I like having control. Suddenly, I was in a world where it seemed I had no control. I spent so much time wishing away the days when my kids were dependent on me for EVERYTHING. I loved marking the stages where they grew in their independence—they graduated from diapers, then they could brush their own teeth, then shower and dress themselves (that was a big one). I was getting some control back and gaining more freedom. I did not embrace those challenging days the way I could have. I was always longing to make a big difference outside of my own home. If only I could (fill in the blank), then I could have a positive influence on others. I could really make a difference in this world.

I spent the next eight years "filling in the blank" with one thing after another. As my daughters grew, I continued to look outside my own home to figure out where I could make the most impact on others. I started a nutritional supplement business, which would allow me to help others with their health. Plus, I got intrigued by the health-care industry. "ObamaCare," as it was known at the time, was skyrocketing healthcare costs, so I got into the health insurance business to help people get into better healthcare plans that would save them money. I even got licensed to sell health insurance. Surely, I could make a ton of money helping people save money on healthcare, while at the same time working with individuals to improve their health through supplementation.

All the while, what I really needed to do was to work on healing my own heart.

On that fateful day in 2014, when I recognized for the first time that I never accepted God as my "boss," my real journey began, digging into who I am and what I am called to do. The process of peeling of my emotional "onion" brought many tears and tough times.

Who Is Your god?

"No one can serve two masters, for either he will hate the one and love the other, or he will be devoted to the one and despise the other. You cannot serve God and money" (Matthew 6:24).

Notice that I spelled "god" with a little "g" and not a big "G". Think about it: what or who do you run to when you are hurting, when things aren't going well in your life? What is your "love" that you run to when things get tough? Is it chocolate? Junk food? Beer? Wine? The hard stuff? Is it a person? Your spouse? Your work? Even pornography? (Yep...I said it.) There is probably someone reading this that answered yes to several of these things. I actually have had a few of these "gods" in my past.

My first love, obviously, was basketball. It was my escape from the yelling and screaming in my home as a child. It was my "happy place." It could be 35 degrees in the cold Ohio winter, but I would go outside with my fingerless gloves and shoot, shoot, shoot. It would get me away from the toxic environment inside my home. It was also my escape from the prison of working at my dad's office building on the weekends. We would have to go take care of all the maintenance on this building. That might not sound bad, but it was such a toxic environment that it was physically and emotionally painful. My basketball practice was right down the street, so I was able to leave and go to my "heaven on earth" in the gym. Basketball was my liberator from the emotional prison. In college, when things weren't going great, I found my solace once again in the quiet gym. I could go shoot for hours by myself. This is where I found my "true self," I thought. That's why every loss tore me apart. My "god" was forsaking me.

By the time I became an Assistant Coach, I had learned to subdue the pain of losing. They stung a bit, but didn't stay with me the way they did as a player. It was easier to justify to myself that it wasn't my fault; It was all on the Head Coach—win or lose. Some of that was ingrained in me by the coaches I worked with; you learn what you live. So, in my Head Coaching days, all the pain of losing roared back under the pressure to win: "it was all me, baby," win or lose. The outcome was all on my shoulders. This was my choice, by the way. Oh, I could give credit to my assistants when we won, but I threw the losses on my own shoulders like an old, cozy blanket. I would snuggle with those suckers. The first year, I gave myself grace because the cupboard was left pretty bare for me. The second year, we were in a building period, just getting some of our own players, so there was still some grace. But by the third year, I felt I was being "forsaken" again by my "god" every time we lost. Things were not getting better and "my god" didn't have any good answers for me.

My second "god" was alcohol.

The drinking started at 13. It was simply social and experimental. I had lots of older siblings who drank, and eventually curiosity got the best of me. It carried on through high school, where it became an escape. It seemed like a great way to hide from emotions I didn't know how to handle. The weekend planning began on Wednesday, as I hunted down where the best parties would be. I usually ended up drinking to the point of passing out, not just a couple of beers. There is a lot I don't remember about that time, and I thank God, as I believe that is a way He has protected me.

The pattern continued through college. There were even more opportunities, because the weekend got rolling on Thursday night at "mug night." On mug night, you could fill your mug, no matter how big, for a dollar. Five dollars could get you pretty hammered. But, of course, "everyone was doing it," so it wasn't a problem. Alcohol was the "friend" that helped me through many struggles. Through my freshman and sophomore years, I had academic problems, so I would run to my "friend." As it turns out, some of my issues were likely the result of spending too much time with my "friend" and not enough time studying. By the grace of God—big "G" again—I didn't become an alcoholic. I graduated with a 3.45 GPA, so at some point, I managed to get control of things. Then, after I got my first coaching job, my alcohol "god" took a back seat to my basketball "god." I still drank, but it was under control and social.

Now for my third "god"... Money. This one reared its ugly head later in my life. Or at least, to a level that I was able to recognize it. After losing my coaching job, with its six-figure income, I felt empty. I was the primary breadwinner of the family, so my job took precedence over anything my husband did. He is a CPA and he was working part-time while I was coaching, doing the "Mr. Mom" act after Molly was born. Later, he went to work full-time and we switched roles. This was so hard for me at first: not only did I get my identity in being a coach, but also was prideful about making a lot of money. My drive became about figuring out how to replace the six-figure income I lost.

I started several businesses, which eventually drove me to the business seminar that introduced me to my big "G" God. I learned that I could not serve more than one master, and the three that I was serving were more important to me than the ONE TRUE GOD. Once I accepted Jesus into my heart, my life drastically changed. My priorities were totally flipped on their head. The new alignment became:

1. Spirit
2. Spouse—the most important earthly relationship
3. Kids
4. Work
5. Money

I'd had it all wrong before. The way it works is, if I have a decision to make, I first find where it fits in the priority list and make sure that it does not trump any of the relationships above it. For example, if I am thinking about getting into a business venture, I have to check it with my priorities. Business and work are #4 on the list. Would getting into that business create a problem in my spiritual life, my relationship with my husband, or my responsibility for my kids? If the answer is yes to any of those questions, then I don't get into the business.

This is a great tool in decision-making and planning. If a potential decision would disrupt the peace in my life, then it's an easy answer. The best part is, because I have a working relationship with my big "G", I get to ask Him His thoughts. If it's not in His plan, the answer is also NO.

Coming Full Circle

Basketball served as my god for a good part of my life. That came crashing down when I got let go from The University of Akron. At that point, basketball became a source of pain in my life, and stayed there for a long time. I didn't watch college basketball games for a couple of years. I know, that seems so extreme, but it's the truth. I associated basketball with the worst pain I had ever experienced. So, it makes sense that I spent about five years chasing business opportunities totally unrelated to basketball, right? My only contact with basketball was coaching my kids, and I only did that because there was no way I would let someone else coach my kids. I had so much basketball knowledge, much more than the average parent could possibly share. These kids would be lucky to have me as a coach. Getting back on the court and teaching young kids the game began to rekindle in me a bit of the fire I'd had throughout my career. My passion to encourage and teach was flickering in my Spirit.

I continued following those other distractions for quite a while. It wasn't until I went to Israel that I finally understood what it meant to be "formed in my mother's womb" (Jeremiah 1:5). I felt the love of My Father in a way I had never felt before. I began to fully understand how much He loved me. He had planted desires in me and designed me with gifts before I was born. I began to understand that basketball was a desire that He placed in me. It was not intrinsically bad. He designed me with the skills to coach and teach and lead. That was not bad, however the way I used them and let them control me had become destructive.

My passion for basketball was validated by my Creator. Understanding this has restored my confidence in the gifts He has given me. My passion for basketball has been rekindled. Now, I can use my coaching experience to relate to coaches and the challenges they face and help them find the richness in the gift they have in coaching. Understanding who you are and the purpose for which you are designed by the great Creator allows you to use your gifts to build up others to work for the greater good and the Glory of God.

4

The Long Road To Healing

IT TURNS out that getting fired finally exposed all the wounds I had never dealt with from my life. I had no idea they went so deep inside me. Each wound grew up from a lie I had accepted about myself. The first step in healing them, as I learned through my study with my coach, Dani Johnson, was to identify the first time that I experienced those lies, in order to get to the root and dig them out. The process can be very painful, but getting to the root and identifying where they started is an important part of the healing process. It is an amazing revelation to discover how to get to the root of the source that led to such beliefs. The ability to cut it off and move forward is worth all of the internal agony you may go through to be free.

You could say that, because those lies were spoken over me by others, I am simply a victim and there is nothing I can do about it. But the truth is that we make the decision to believe that lie and then it manifests in our actions throughout our lives. I chose to believe each lie and allowed it to take root deep inside of me. I had a part to play, and I have to own it.

Once you uncover the first time you received the lie about yourself, you must forgive the person responsible (it may even be yourself), release and bless that person. Release any bitterness held in your heart toward that person. Only when you have completed this process to forgive, release, and bless them can you be free from the stronghold that lie has over your life.

Rejection and Abandonment

One of my biggest wounds was in the area of rejection and abandonment. Of course, when you get fired it is natural to feel rejected and abandoned, not good enough. I started by forgiving, releasing, and blessing the new athletic director. He was an easy target to identify and forgive. But getting fired wasn't the root of my sense of rejection, it just exposed the tree of rejection I had allowed to grow inside my heart.

To really get to the root, I had to go back deep into my childhood, to the rejection from my dad. My dad's anger and rage created an unhealthy environment. His moving to Florida was a healthy absence in our home. Even though I was thankful he was gone, this still created a the void of having a loving father-figure in my life. As a result I felt unloved and rejected. This for sure affected other areas of my life, particularly the longing for approval from others. I had years of built up pain from feeling unwanted by my own father. Getting to the root of this was so liberating.

I now have a better understanding of why my siblings all went as far away from home that they could as soon as they had the chance. Because of our home life, we all went into survival mode: we each had to deal with the pain we went through in our own ways. We were all so wounded that we had no idea how to reach out to others in their pain. Being the youngest, I just followed what everyone else did, which was to hide ourselves in our own lives. That meant not talking about what we were going through. It was the elephant in the room that nobody wanted to talk about. Getting away from it and staying away seemed to be the best way to handle it. This for sure contributed to my independence, but it also led to more feelings of abandonment by my siblings.

I continued to dig deep to reveal the experiences and people that abandoned me. I went down the list forgiving, releasing and blessing each one. It was liberating then and still is today.

Forgiveness

Forgiving my dad and all who had abandoned me in my childhood was so important to my healing. I had to go through the list of everyone who had hurt me in my past and go through the steps of forgiving them. I also had to take responsibility for my own feelings and the beliefs that I accepted. It was important to first identify the hurt, put a face to it, and work through the forgiveness exercise I had learned. There were several siblings that really wounded me emotionally. I addressed my feelings with them and how their words and actions had affected me. I forgave them and in return asked forgiveness for the judgment that I had placed on them. There are always two sides to every story. I was able to forgive them and receive forgiveness, as well as ask God's blessing on them. Our relationships today are stronger as a result.

Evicting Anger

Next, I had to tackle anger, which was a big part of my personality. I would get angry and yell and cuss when pressure was on me. I would erupt like a principality of darkness and go into a verbal rage. It was flat-out ugly. I really thought it was genetic. Dad was physically and verbally abusive to Mom. I have many memories of coming home from school, walking around the corner to our house and his raging voice booming down the street. "Couldn't you close the windows?" I would think to myself. I would enter the house because I didn't know what else to do. I was 8 years old. I would see plates, cups, anything in his path, soaring across the kitchen and crashing into the fireplace.

Anger seemed to be a family trait passed down to all of us. My brothers and sisters manifested this rage, as well. We each seemed to have our own sparring partner growing up. Mine was my brother Keith. It seemed that we would end up fighting over the littlest things. Yes, siblings argue. But, this was physical rage. I was so angry at him one time I punched him in the face and knocked his tooth out. Anger HAD to be genetic. It was the only explanation at the time.

It made sense to me when I learned that anger is the result of unhealed heart issues, but it hit me like a ton of bricks. We had so many unhealed wounds of the heart from our childhood. Anger wasn't genetic, it was a result of our common painful experiences. When I was able to identify my roots of anger from my past, I was able to dig them out. My heart began to heal and the times that I got angry continued to decrease. Now it is a rare occasion rather than the normal reaction. I have learned to live in the Spirit rather than the flesh, and that living in the Spirit produces fruit; love, joy, peace, patience, kindness, gentleness, goodness and to me most importantly, self-control.

The Hardest Person To Forgive

As strange as it might sound, the hardest person to forgive in this whole process was myself. As I looked back at my career at Akron, and as the pressure built and the problems with my staff got bigger and bigger, my anger grew and grew. I could remember a few times that I unleashed on the team in the locker room and my staff in the hallway at halftime. I was a complete mess and it was not pretty. I am sure this was one reason for my firing, as I'm sure the players shared my raging with the new AD. He never did say why—he simply said there is no cause for your getting let go—but deep down, I had a feeling that the players were involved in my getting let go. I knew the truth about my own actions and am not proud of my lack of self-control.

This was a hard truth for me to admit to myself. Whew! The truth shall make you free!!! It took me years to learn this. I had a lot of conversations with God about my anger and asking His forgiveness. I am so thankful that He is a loving and forgiving God. After all, that is why He sent His son for sinners like me. WOW! That is amazing. So, I attempted to reach out to some of my former players to ask forgiveness. It was humbling and liberating—and really hard to do. The freedom and peace that I gained from that exercise of humility was amazing—even if they did not respond.

How Insecurity Manifests

As I am writing this book, the news of Kobe Bryant's death just hit the news. It turns out that Kobe was Catholic. I had just read again about his infidelity story and how he met with a priest to help him to change his ways. The funny thing is, I had many times thought of going to meet with my parish priest as I felt things getting out of control. I chose not to because I did not want to reveal my personal struggles to anyone. It would expose me. I saw it as weakness. I would rather keep it to myself and deal with the outcome. That ended up being a bad choice. I wish I had the courage to take that step back then. If I knew then what I know now, I would have drawn courage from Isaiah 41:10: "Fear not, for I am with you; be not dismayed, for I am your God; I will strengthen you, I will help you, I will uphold you with my righteous right hand."

There were other times in my career that I could remember my fear of rejection, or not being good enough, manifesting itself. One time, I was in a staff meeting, talking about defensive strategy. Defense was my strength, and I knew how to teach it, because I had learned from some great teachers and our teams had had success in this area. We had just come off of a conference championship season, playing the defense the way we had been teaching it. We were talking about the proper technique for closing out. There was a new coach on staff that was challenging me on how to teach the technique of close outs. I took this so personally that I actually got in an argument with her over it. It sounds silly now, I know. I felt that she was challenging everything I knew about coaching in that one instance. I flew off the handle and stood my ground as if there was only one way to do it and it was MINE.

What was really showing through was my insecurities.

At one point in my career, I replaced a coach who, before she left, told the players that I "wasn't good enough for this job." Of course, it didn't take long for that comment to filter down to me. I guess I shouldn't have been surprised by it. This kind of thing happens. The problem was that I let it into my head and I began to believe it until my actions reflected my beliefs. Those seeds of rejection that were planted in my childhood were being watered by this new seed that was planted in me because I chose to believe it. Once a seed is planted, it starts to grow roots unless it is rooted out. Think of the weeds you pull up in your backyard: if you don't pull them out all the way down to the root, what happens? They come back deeper and stronger and can spread to create more weeds.

My own insecurities continued to feed my feelings of self-doubt, which then grew into resentment toward the new coach. Instead of humbling myself to learn from someone new and be open to new ideas, I stood my ground and dug my heels in more. I needed to be right, no questions asked.

My fear of rejection led to self-doubt, which grew into bitterness toward her. I felt that she was attacking me personally. This delusion added to my insecurity. It was a vicious cycle that I kept in the back of my mind in my dealings with her. Now, keep in mind it was my choice to interpret this situation this way and to receive the negativity that was growing inside of me. It was my choice to stew on these thoughts and make room for the resulting bitterness and unforgiveness.

When I learned what bitterness and unforgiveness do in the body and mind, I was blown away. "Persistent bitterness may result in global feelings of anger and hostility that, when strong enough, could affect a person's physical health," said psychologist Dr. Carsten Wrosch. Both of these emotions trigger cascades of neurotransmitters that flood the body and gradually break down internal organs. They literally kill you over time.

It's worth pointing out here how many times I have used the word, "felt." I am amazed, as I look back, at how many times I allowed my feelings to direct my action. As my coach, Dani, often says, "feelings often lie." Your feelings can distort things so badly that you start to believe that love is hate and kindness is manipulation. Trust your instincts, but never your feelings. Feelings will lie to you. They lied to me.

Learning how to identify these feelings of bitterness and unforgiveness that rooted themselves in my heart was an incredible gift. Taking the next step to root it out and leave it behind is perhaps the most valuable skill I have ever developed. Learning to forgive, release and bless others (and myself) has been life-changing and may have added years to my life.

You may have guessed this, but this process is biblical. 1 Peter 3:9 says "not paying back evil for evil or insult for insult, on the contrary, giving a blessing." I have learned how to exercise this practice with my daughters and husband, to model the behavior and ask forgiveness when I mess up (which I do frequently) and to show them how to go through this process with one another when they hurt each other. It is an important life skill and it has changed the atmosphere in my home.

Rooting Out Shame

Digging even deeper into my past to find the roots that got triggered when I got fired was an ongoing process. I had to unveil all the deep-seeded roots that led to my near breakdown. I had hit rock bottom. The scars of my past had been scraped open like I'd had a bad fall off a bicycle. Jesus had "taken the wheel," but little did I know the winding path He would take me down. And this was only the beginning. I spent the years from 2014 to 2019 in the process of repairing my mind, body, and soul, and I'm still working through it. He has been doing this work in me, but I have been so willing to get down to it that I have been a willing participant. I am tired of living a life of shame and embarrassment.

"You are not the person you were, but the person you became because of your circumstances." As I started to reflect on this statement, I looked back at my career to see what circumstances began to change me. I think it started in earnest at Iowa State. It was a higher pressure situation where you had to produce or get fired. Talk about other coaches and how they should be fired was such casual talk. It was normal conversation among coaches. But it's reality: win, produce, or get fired.

I began to feel the pressure of producing at Iowa State. This was definitely more of a self-inflicted pressure than an external pressure. After all, The Cyclones had just come off of an "Elite 8" finish the year before. I took the place of a coach who went on to be a Head Coach, so I had big shoes to fill.

My responsibilities were focused on scouting opponents and recruiting, feeding the pipeline for the future. On my first scout assignment, I was actually pretty intimidated. Those seeds of "you're not good enough for this level" planted long ago started to poke their roots into the ground. I worked with the other assistant to be sure that my scouting report met the expectations. As it turned out, I did the scout quite well. I passed my first test, but had my doubts going into it.

Those seeds of doubt were hidden for quite a while. My good friend left the staff. Her departure left me feeling very vulnerable, as she was my connection to that job. I had a good working relationship with Coach Bill, but, I fell short in really getting deeper into fully learning all I could about him and from him. Knowing what I know now, I can see it was my fear of showing my vulnerabilities that kept me from asking, learning, and growing. I was very good with the surface, fun, keep-it-loose conversations. We could go and have a beer and small talk, but when it came to really going deeper, I fell short. I felt like I had to know everything there was to know and to not show weakness at this level. I was very foolish.

When the new assistant came in, she had a clean slate and no relationships with anyone. She had been a Head

Coach at the NAIA level and had been successful there. She came in with her own experiences and had a lot to share. However, we butted heads a bit when it came to basketball knowledge—my pride caused me to dig my heels into the ground when we disagreed, rather than being open to learn, and that created tension we didn't need. Those roots of "you're not good enough" started to go deeper. In trying to defend myself, I really lost out on personal growth. Rather than taking in what I could learn, I wanted to prove that I knew better.

I share this because now I am able to identify my actions for what they were: fear and self-doubt. They had rooted themselves so deeply inside me and were hidden for so long, that when I was challenged, they showed themselves, although I didn't recognize it then. If I had known then what I know now, I might still be coaching at a high level today, but that is not my story.

The Root of Brokenness

We are all broken in some way. Even the most spiritual people we know have experienced brokenness. Some have overcome the brokenness in their lives, while some are still soaking in it, marinating in bitterness, self-doubt, or the fear of failure that is keeping them from being the best they can be. For most of us - myself included - brokenness goes deep into the core of who we are. Like most people, I was able to mask it at different times in my life and to different degrees. But as we've already seen, it finds ways of poking through to the surface and shows at the most inopportune moments.

I have actually experienced two cycles of brokenness in my life: the first cycle was in my childhood, while the second has been in my adulthood and professional life.

The brokenness of my childhood was rooted in me by my

home-life. I have opened the window of that pain to allow you to peer through it. To most people, it looked like I had it all together: I was a success in the classroom, a student leader, a good athlete, and making my mark on the basketball court. The truth was that I was as messed-up as a kid could be.

I started drinking during the summer before eighth grade and it quickly became a habit. I was hanging out with some kids that had the same interests. It all seemed pretty innocent, but looking back, it was so deceptive. After all, I was a good church-going kid (wink, wink). It wasn't long before I moved past the "social drinker" stage and got really good at numbing out of reality. Come Monday, I would be back to being a brown-nose, goody-two-shoes at school. The teachers loved me and would have been appalled to know what the Phi Beta Kappa was doing every weekend.

Thankfully, my mom was praying and God was watching over me. I don't believe that He approved of my behavior, but I do believe that He was covering me in His protection. I firmly believe that He did not allow me to get caught in my ways, as it wasn't quite time for the "big old butt-whooping" that I deserved—that would come much later.

History Only Repeats Itself If You Let It

I was talking to a very good coaching friend of mine, sharing with her about writing a book, when I opened up about the pain I felt from being fired. She could relate; she had been fired from a job, too. We began a discussion about what drives coaches to coach and came to the conclusion that there are different drivers at different levels of coaching. We also realized that someone's past experience can direct their drive. I asked her what her motivator was and she told me it was the fear of getting fired again. I could feel her anxiety welling up inside me. Heck, one of the reasons I stayed away from getting back to coaching at a high level was the fear of failure.

Lately, I have been giving that more thought. History will only repeat itself if you let it. When bad things happen, such as losing a job, you can choose to let them fester and burrow a root of fear in your soul, or you can choose to learn and grow from them, and maybe prevent it from happening again. That's easier said than done, for sure.

To do this, you need to take a good, honest look at why you lost your job. It took me years to get up the courage to be 100% honest with myself. The truth was hard to face, but I had to acknowledge that I was ultimately responsible for getting fired from my coaching position. Did outside factors weigh in on this? Sure, there were some. But if I want to grow, then the buck has to stop here with me. Once I was able to take an honest look in the mirror, I could see my weaknesses and where I had fallen short. At that point, I became coachable. I grew to know myself better and to improve in those areas of weakness. It started with a lot of forgiveness.

As I grew in faith and a deeper understanding of God's love that drives out fear, I came to the understanding that His love had helped me to conquer my fear of failure. It still creeps in now and then, but I can identify it for what it is and call it out. I am stronger for having gone through the fire, and can move forward, trusting in the fact that His hand is upon me.

I messed up when I was not walking with God, and I learned from it. I put my faith (and my fear) in all the wrong things. Now I know that, if I fall, He is with me. There is so much peace in that.

My doubts and fears of not being good enough have been wiped away. I look at failure as an opportunity to grow and refine myself. I am in no hurry to go back to the pressures of Division I coaching, but I also know that I am not being motivated by fear, but rather by obedience. If I sensed that my Heavenly Father wanted me to go back to that life, I could step out in faith that He has called and equipped me to be successful at it. You can't pressure me to go back with fear, and you couldn't pressure me to stay out. The enemy feeds fear to keep you from being the amazing person that God designed you to be, so you can't allow fear to direct your actions. When you sense fear, acknowledge it and renounce its right to steer you. Be the best you can be, FEARLESS AND FREE!

Redeemed

Since 2014, when I started this faith journey, I have peeled back many layers of self and uncovered some undesirable parts of myself. Fortunately, I am not a finished product, but rather a work-in-progress.

Constantly.

In March of 2019, I had the opportunity to go to Israel. It was a Biblical journey through several areas, starting in the desert, entering the promised land, and finally walking where Jesus walked as He fulfilled His mission on the Earth. During that trip, I wrote in my journal, "I am here in Israel to gain a full understanding of who I am as a daughter of the Most High, Elohim" (which is God's name in Hebrew). "My Father loves me and wants to give me the desires of my heart. It's really quite simple that I trust in my Father. He has my hand through all the good and all the trials I will face. But ultimately, His blessings are upon me."

While I was there, I got the opportunity to dig deeply into who I was as a person after struggling for so long with my coaching identity. The beautiful thing that He showed me in Israel was that He put the desire to coach in my heart. He created me to help kids, to teach, and to lead through my passion for basketball. I love working with young athletes and helping them with the mental and physical aspects of the game. It is an incredible blessing, and it is God's gift to me. Once I got that revelation, I felt free to go back home and joyfully live the life He designed for me. I felt like the healing process was accelerated in that time, so I could move forward in peace and walk in love. It is so liberating to be in this place. The best part is that now, I know that He is guiding my every step. I have no worries about winning games, because I coach for His Glory, and I know I am doing His work.

The very first day on the bus in Israel, our tour leader, Dani, explained that shepherding was the theme for that trip. "If you can be a shepherd," she said, "you can be a good coach." I just smiled as I recognized God giving me His confirmation of why I was on that trip. He loves Me! This was also where He confirmed for me to write about my transformation. Jesus is the Good Shepherd.

The Shepherd Coach

Just weeks before going to Israel, I read the book *Shepherd Coach*, by Tom Roy. It was the catalyst that got to me to go back to the James A Rhodes Arena (the JAR)—the very same gym I had been fired from to complete my healing process. The book really wrecked me, especially the first chapter, which talked about coaching as a God-given gift. It talked about why we coach and made me reflect on my past. I thought I had dealt with all the pain and was free of the bondage. But as I broke down in tears I realized there were still feelings that I had not dealt with.

I immediately called Tom and shared with him what I was feeling. He asked me if I had been back to the JAR. I had not. He told me I needed to return to experience the complete healing. Growing up in the Catholic church (and the Catholic Youth Organization) we didn't really learn about having a relationship with God. I know that I am where I am today because of the revelation I received in 2014. I don't want my kids or the kids I coach to grow up saying, "nobody ever told me." This is why I started "Champion Athletes for Christ" for sixth, seventh, and eighth graders at St Hilary in 2016. Our youth ministry leader and I meet with the kids every two weeks to discuss how we can be Jesus to others in sports. It is so awesome to hear them talk about God. And although some of the kids are so much more expressive than others, the beauty is that the kids keep coming back every week. There are about 40 kids between the three groups, and as we are guided by the Holy Spirit, we get to drip the love of God into them in the 25 minutes we get with them each time.

Why, Today and Everyday, I am So Thankful

Our significance in life is not about what appears on the outside, but what is reflected from the inside. What is the condition of your heart?

It's easy to focus on making sure the outside looks good by putting on a smile and a nice outfit, but what is on the inside which is coming out of your mouth? In Matthew 12:34, Jesus says, "...for the mouth speaks from the overflow of the heart."

Anger came out of me when I was under pressure, as the overflow of my unhealed heart spoke through my words. I was not presenting my best self, that's for sure. I am thankful that I found a coach in Dani Johnson that helped me uncover the root of my brokenness and brought out the best in me. She pressed me to dig deeper and to lean in to my Heavenly Father.

I am also thankful I found the love of Jesus and the commitment of my Maker. Colossians 3:2 says, "set your mind on the things above, not on earthly things," and that is what I endeavor to do. I live for an audience of ONE. If I focus on pleasing God and glorifying Him in all that I do, I don't need to worry about the outcome. I may stumble and fall, but as I choose to look up and find my strength in God, I rest in the fact that everything will work out.

It makes life so much simpler. Life is a roller coaster with ups and downs, twists and turns (I may even throw up now and again), but I know that He is with me at every creak and jolt. He will be there to hold the can when I toss my cookies, and to help clean up the mess. He "took the wheel" from me when I came crashing to a halt in 2006, and gingerly led me back to Him.

Living in gratitude and thanksgiving in the tough times, as well as the good times, has changed my life for the better.

You Can't Judge a Book by Its Cover

Growing up "a good Catholic girl," and doing all the "right things," I was putting on a good show, but what was in my heart? In reality, I was a real mess, but it was a hidden mess. I was able to forge through the messiness of my childhood, pushing the "crap" I had built up inside back up into the corners of my mind. Think of it as a storage closet in the basement, all those taped-up boxes of stuff that you carry with you each time you move, although you don't know why. It remains in those boxes, packed away until you hit a point that it gets so moldy that it needs to be cleaned out.

I was recently participating in a bible study by Pastor Craig Groeschel called "Dangerous Prayers." It challenged me to think about the condition of my heart. I always believed my heart was good, since I went to church and wasn't trying to hurt anyone. I lived my life with good intentions. The prophet Jeremiah once said, "The human heart is the most deceitful of all things, and desperately wicked. Who really knows how bad it is?" (Jeremiah 17:9)

OUCH! at hit me between the eyes.

In that Bible study, I read: "as humans, we are really about self—not Christ. It's about what's temporary—not eternal...It's obsessed with what we want not what God wants." Without God and that strong connection to God our hearts are very selfish. The only way to know God's ways and to walk in His ways is to let Him in. He will not force His way in as He is a gentleman.

The truth about me was that I was going through the motions of faith. I went to church but never felt like I was connecting with God. I knew all the prayers and could pray them but it was not in my heart. I was not transformed by the Word of God, I was simply doing my "duty" as a Catholic and fulfilling my Sunday obligation. What was being professed at Church was not manifesting in my heart because I did not have a true relationship with my Heavenly Father. So, what happened? As things started to get tougher at Akron my pride and ego set in. I was going to fix things by sheer will of my own. My motives were very self-centered and focused on the win column. If I focused on the relationships and connecting with the hearts of my team things may have worked out differently. I did not seek wise counsel as the Bible teaches. I even thought about going to talk to a priest for guidance, but I never did. I needed courage to make some really hard changes in the program but I did not have the courage to do it.

As I am writing this we are going through the COVID-19 pandemic. The whole world is practicing "social distancing." We have been given a "stay at home order" by our state government and most states are following the same order. This has caused churches to offer only online services. There is "social distancing" from congregating in large crowds. I would consider myself growing up as "socially distanced" from God. On the surface, I was all about God when I went to church. That's what people could see. I was not inviting Him into my heart. I did not know how to have that personal relationship with my Father. This kept me from truly living out the goodness that my heart intended.

I was given the opportunity at Akron to realize the dream, the desire that was planted in my heart by my creator. I did not actively pursue a relationship with the Creator. Relying on my own strength and understanding and making decisions based on my own thoughts. I was ignoring the warning signs that were going off like sirens that led to my own sin and destruction. I placed my thoughts and opinions on that of my fellow man not on what God values. Things all came crashing down and that basement of mine got flooded with the monsoon of anger from losing my job. All the hidden "crap" came floating around me. The bitterness, the shame of abandonment, anger, fear, unforgiveness, all came pouring out. I had hit the bottom. What appeared to be good was exploding into a mess.

How do you get to that relationship with God when you feel so lost? It starts with the transforming of your mind and heart. To start to read His word on your own and to understand that God the Father sent Jesus to live a human life. Jesus understands the human struggles. By his stripes we are healed, forgiven.

Know that He wants you more than anything. Step by step one day at a time learning and growing and reading His word, the Bible. It's a process but you can stand firm and make that commitment now to our Lord and Savior. Then work at it as Michelangelo worked at creating his sculpture, "David." When asked how he created the famous sculpture he is quoted as saying, "It is easy. You just chip away the stone that doesn't look like David." So, simply ask God to help you identify what is not of His goodness in your heart and chip away at it one day at a time. As it says in Hebrews 16:32 "out of weakness we are made strong." Take your weaknesses to Him and He will make you strong. God doesn't see us in our moment of sin, He sees us as what we can become.

Humility

One night a few years ago, I was lying in bed, talking to my husband about the rough day he had just ended. He said he felt like he was falling short in his job. He is a partner on the audit side of a good-sized accounting firm and does some tax work as well. He was frustrated as he was getting questions from clients that he had to ask other team members for guidance. He didn't "know it all". I tried to reassure him, saying, "that is what a team does. You don't need to know all the answers, but you had the humility to ask others for help to deliver the best answer to your client."

I made an analogy of when I was a Head Coach. I felt like I had to have all the answers and know more than my assistants in every area of the game, but that was foolish pride. I did not have the humility to ask for help or to give my assistants enough freedom to be strong in areas where I was weak. I also had a "need" to be in control, which obviously didn't end well for me. In my mind, to ask for help was to show weakness and expose my lack in areas.

The most successful people I know today have said the same thing: you don't want to be the smartest person in the room. Surround yourself with people who know more than you, and continue to learn and grow, and you will be unusually successful. That, my friend, takes humility...and is BRILLIANT.

The definition of humility is "a modest or low view of one's own importance." Here is what the Bible says about humility: "When pride comes, then comes disgrace, but with humility comes wisdom." Proverbs 11:2, and the humble are raised up in God's eyes. "Humble yourselves before the Lord, and he will lift you up." James 4:10.

When pride comes, then comes disgrace. Oh my, how true this is. My pride at Iowa State in wanting to be right was so glaring in my desire for recognition for the knowledge I had. The disgrace there was in weakening relationships with others. It hurt me in the bigger picture of life. My pride got in the way of the person that loved people, that loved making people laugh, that loved embracing every moment for the goodness that was in it. My personal pride began to erode that part of me. My lack of humility put me on the eager track to become a Head Coach.

Becoming a Head Coach would put me in control. It would raise me up to a new level of respect. The perceived respect of the title of Head Coach was so appealing to me. I did feel that I was prepared to handle all of the challenges of being a Head Coach. I had learned from my mentors and thought about what was good to take with me and what I wanted to leave behind. If I could take all the good and put it into practice from all three programs, I would surely be a success.

I went to Akron with the best of intentions. I saw the mess the program was in with division III transfers that were now on scholarship and the drug infestation and was excited that the only direction to go was up. I spent a lot of time early on with the players that I had. Working to improve them on the court and create a sense of pride in the program. Cleaning up mess after mess as I went along. It was really a big disaster to be honest.

The program started to look like a division I program. The problem was that I stopped growing myself. I had a good idea of how to get things done and was doing it my way.

More, more, more...*that* was the answer. Work harder. Spend more time on film. Work the kids harder. That had to be the answer.

But this takes me right back to my past mistakes of holding on to pride. I didn't reach out to my mentors to ask for help. I did rely on my assistants for input, of course, but what we were doing wasn't working. I should have reached out to an unbiased point of view. But, that would expose my weakness. Where did this idea that I had to have all the answers come from? One of the Head Coaches I worked for told me week one on the job "I don't need any help with the X's and O's. Your job is to recruit." Remember that words are seed. That seed was planted in me years ago and took root when I was a Head Coach.

The lesson here is to keep on growing. Look into the mirror and ask yourself, what can I do better today? If you are not sure, find a trusted friend that will be honest with you and tell you.

What I was doing at Akron was not working and a change needed to be made. It just took me a long time to be honest with myself.

I failed in that position at Akron as the Head Coach. What I did with that failure was to accept it as the overall truth, that I was a terrible coach. I let that failure define me. This was complete foolishness. Did I fail? Yes. Did that negate all the good I had done to get to that position? No. Did I choose to accept that failure as my truth? Yes.

I actually just came to this realization the other day. I was having a conversation with a friend about a business failure she had. She had an idea for a business and started it from scratch. She realized just a few months into it that she had problems. She overlooked a key piece, the ability to take something good and mass produce it. She didn't have the ability to mass produce, which led to failure of the business.

As a result, she is terribly afraid to start another business. The fear of failure has gripped her so hard that she doesn't want to try again.

I talked to her about the failure and asked her what she learned. Turns out she learned a lot about running a business. The mistakes she made opened her eyes to what she would need to do before starting the next business. Perhaps a bit more due diligence before jumping in. Does her failure in that business define her ability to succeed in her next venture? Absolutely not. She learned many lessons from her stumble.

For me, the same applies. Does failure in my first Head Coaching job define how I would be in my next? I should say not. I have learned so much from that failure. It has taken me many years of digging. Did I fail at that coaching job? Overall, yes. I did not have a good record. I did a terrible job at hiring and managing my staff. This trickled into the management of the relationships of the players, which is where the biggest downfall was. I lost sight of the most important facet of being a coach. My job was to teach these young ladies what it would take to be successful after basketball. I am so sorry to say that I fell terribly short at Akron in my role as the Head Coach.

Does that mean that I was a complete failure at doing that in every position I held before that? Absolutely not. I actually did a pretty solid job of that in my previous roles. The pressure and the fog of all that I had going on around me clouded my vision of what I was meant to do in that season, in that time.

We all will have storms in our lives. How we come out of the storm is what is important. I guess that is another reason I am writing this, to help others get out of the storm they may be in faster than I did. Learn from my mistakes. What I have learned has helped me to more clearly see when others are going through storms and have fog that needs clearing. I love drawing the analogies from other peoples' struggles, like my friend's or my husband's, and using what I have learned to help them through theirs. Humility is the best possible tool to have. To think higher of others than you do yourself will help you to reach your highest dreams.

James 1:22-25 is a good reminder:

"And become doers of the Word and not hearers only, deceiving yourselves. Because if anyone was a hearer of the Word and not a doer, he is like a man who looks at his natural face in the mirror, for he looks at himself and goes away, and immediately forgets what he was like."

Unbelief

I love learning and growing. I have spent more time working on myself than anything else over the past six years. Some might say I am a slow learner, but the truth is it's just a never-ending process. The deeper I dig the greater the revelation of what happened to me at Akron to spiral me down the way I did. I learned a lot of unbelief.

Unbelief is the enemy driving a wedge into my thoughts and kicking up self-doubt. In the movie, "Justice League," the mean and ugly flying insects represent evil. When they smelled fear, they attacked that person in their weakness. This is exactly what Satan is doing when he senses the slightest bit of unbelief in a person. He preys on that, stirring up self-doubt and feeding your thoughts with lies. Those thoughts produce more negative behavior, which then becomes a constant cycle of destruction.

The seeds of doubt were planted in my past. They sprouted and bore fruit with every loss at Akron, until the harvest began to weigh on me. It was like the whacking of a hammer on a nail: loss, wack, loss, wack, loss, wack, wack, wack, until the wedge of unbelief totally penetrated my thoughts. It stirred up all the hurt and shame that had been lying dormant since I was a kid—the fear of rejection, of loss, of not being enough. All the lies of my past were swirling around and I didn't know how to stop them.

If I had known then what I know now, I would have recognized the lies for what they were. In my weakness, I need to identify what I am feeling and call it what it is: the enemy drawing me away from all that is good in God. In the past, the lies were truth to me. They were deeply seeded in my being. They led to negative thoughts and fed my anger about my past.

I learned this acronym from my Revelation Wellness classes. When you are sinking in the sea of lies of the enemy, build a B.O.A.T.:

B. Breathe and just Be. The spirit of life and peace is with you. Breathe it in. Let it flood over you.

O. Observe. Become observant of what you are feeling and where you are in your life. Detach from the worries that are troubling you. Step back and be aware of all that is around you.

A. Acknowledge. Identify your fears and don't ignore your feelings. The feelings are real, but you need to understand where they are coming from. If they are good they are of God, if they are negative they are from the enemy. He wants to come into your life and steal and destroy. As you identify the feelings you can disarm the negativity around them.

T. Transform. Change the feelings from negative to positive. Get a vision of the success you desire and come back into the good things that God wants for you.

For a great example of transforming from negative to positive, I think of Wonder Woman. I just love those movies.

So powerful. I envision the look she has when she is ready to kick the enemy's butt. She tilts her head and furrows her brow a bit. I see this as the transformation from "Can I do this?" to "Sorry sucker! You haven't got a chance!" The beauty of drawing strength from the Creator is the ability to look through the lens of Jesus' eyes; to transform troubles into endless possibilities of God's favor. With God on your side, you have the advantage over the principalities and systems of this world. By the blood of Jesus, we have the power over the troubles around us.

"Jesus, Take the Wheel"

One moment, I was in my car, bawling my eyes out and asking Jesus to take the wheel. The next moment, I was unemployed. For years, I believed that Jesus took the wheel by removing me from my coaching job. It was only recently that I received the most profound revelation about it. Are you ready for it?

I actually got fired on my own, by my own actions. Jesus had nothing to do with me losing my job, He took the wheel by catching me after I fell.

I have been so aware of people asking the question, "why does God let bad things happen to good people?" I have pondered this many times myself. There is no explanation that will make everyone happy. As I believe it, God doesn't let things happen, they just happen. Sure, God could micromanage every single thing that happens in our lives. He could control every decision we make, or the actions we take, but He doesn't. God gave us a free will: the freedom to make our own choices and to live life how we want to live it. He wants us to enjoy life and have pleasures in life.

We live in the flesh, and will die in the flesh. Disease, heartache, illness, drug use, car accidents, job loss, and all the bad things you can list are all part of living here on earth; they are all part of the "human effect," as I call it. They are all somehow related to the choices that we as humans make in the flesh. There is always a cause and effect of every choice and decision that we make, and sometimes the outcomes are unpleasant. First Corinthians 6:12 says, "Everything is permissible, but not everything is beneficial" (BSB).

God has a hand in all that we do, whether we are believers or not. Even non-believers have people praying for them, and God is listening. Can he "fix" everything? YES. But that isn't necessarily how HIS plan is to be carried out. Ultimately, His plan will be carried out. Each one of our stories is already written.

I recently questioned God about this very thing. My 12-year-old daughter was ill, to the point that she was admitted to the hospital with Stevens Johnson Syndrome (SJS). SJS is an exaggerated reaction to a virus or antibiotic that attacks the mucous membranes of the body. In some cases, it is fatal. When she was admitted, we were told it would get worse before it got better. I asked the doctor how long we would be in the hospital, and his answer was, "as long as it takes." That's a pretty scary answer for the parents, let alone for a 12-year- old to hear. It was all the more horrifying because the doctors had limited information about this rare disease. There are only about 20,000 cases in the entire United States per year, so it is difficult to research and study. There was so much uncertainty around it.

As I spent 11 days in the Children's Hospital, watching my daughter suffer through the pain of this illness, I came to the realization that God doesn't "let this happen"—it is part of our trials in this human life—but He is there, walking through it with us.

My only choice in that hospital was to lean on and trust in God to help me and my family through this worldly struggle.

As scary as the situation was at times, I was never afraid. That sounds crazy, but it is true. I relied heavily on Romans 8:28, which says, "We know that all things work for good for those who love God, who are called according to His purpose" (NET).

Incidentally, that verse is referring to each person who chooses to follow Him. I knew deep in my heart that God had Finley in the palm of His hand and would heal her from this crazy illness; it was just a matter of time. So, my job was to be a source of strength for my girl every single day in that hospital. On my own, I did not have the strength. I got my strength in knowing that something, someone way bigger than me had this thing all worked out.

That dark moment is part of her story, and it will make sense someday, because good will come of it. The strength that she showed in that battle was above and beyond anything she ever imagined she could do.

That is something she and I will never forget.

Finley's battle was with SJS and it took her 11 days to get through it. My battle was with losing my job and identity, but it has taken me 12 years to break through it. Just as Jesus was at the wheel in the hospital, He has been with me through my healing process. The thing is, I have taken a long time getting in and fastening my seatbelt.

In 2006, I wasn't even on the tricycle when it came to my walk with God. I was a church-going Catholic. I prayed in church, but that was about as far as it went. Since then, He has taken me on a journey of finding my true self. I had to be stripped of who I thought I was—my identity was as a coach. He didn't strip me of that; I did a darned good job of that all by myself. What He did then was He used my fleshly desires to lead me back to Him. It is incredible to look back at my faith journey and how the guidance of the Holy Spirit has brought me to where I am today.

5

The X's and O's of Success

AS COACHES, we gauge success on the wins and losses. In order to win, you must be well prepared and then execute your game plan to overcome the opponent. You also have to know your strengths and weaknesses, and how to arrange your game around them.

At Oregon, we were very good at the technical aspects of defending and applying that to the opponent. I would sit with Coach Litz, who did the defensive schemes for every scouting report, for hours before games, going over what we needed to do. Now, he was VERY meticulous about the scouting report. He went over every detail over, and over, and over, and over. His process was meticulous and very effective. We often led the PAC 10 in defensive categories, like Field Goal Percentage Defense.

At TCU, Coach Mike had more of an offensive mindset, adding sets to get our best players in positions to score. We had the great Sutton twins that were like peanut butter and jelly, milk and cookies, Sonny and Cher, Captain and Tennille... They worked together beautifully. Each of them could anticipate the other's move before she made it. We didn't have great quickness to help us win on the defensive end, so we had to outscore our opponents every game. The greatest game we had was a three-point-fest against our crosstown rival, SMU. It was an epic battle that saw us edge out the Mustangs 127 - 125, with every possible ounce of effort spilled all over the court.

Iowa State was similar to TCU in the fact that we were not the quickest team around, but we had a three-point arsenal beyond comparison.

Coach Fennelly's philosophy was to play a 2-3 match-up and throw in junk defenses to wreak havoc on the offense. Keep the ball out of the paint, rebound and go. We got the ball up the court with great efficiency and would tally threes at record pace.

We had four players on the court at all times that were deadly from downtown (if you're not familiar, that's basketball jargon for shooters who are effective at long shots). I learned how to implement "junk defenses" successfully and became very good at strategizing. Take away their best couple of players and make the rest beat you. This worked out in our favor more often than not. We finished my three seasons there with two Big XII Tournament Championships, one Big XII Conference Championship, and three NCAA Tournament Appearances, resulting in two Sweet Sixteen finishes.

People Skills

I was very good at scouting reports and game plans. I learned this skill from working with many very good coaches in my career. But while game planning is one piece of the success puzzle, people skills is the other piece. As an assistant, my relationships with the players were very important. There were always challenges, but I had good relationships with most of the players.

At each school there always seemed to be one that was in special need of some kind of extra help, and I would take the extra effort to help that kid out. I have always had a heart for the kids that struggle, maybe because I grew up feeling like the underdog. Somehow, I got the idea planted in my head that there were more than just physical differences between Division I athletes and Division III athletes. What I discovered through the years is that an athlete is an athlete. The Division I kids had more skill and spent more time with their sport, but the mentality was no different. The game was the game, it was just played at a faster pace at the Division I level. Kids are kids, no matter where you are in the country or what school you coach. You do your best as a coach to help in whatever way you can.

While I was at Oregon, our top point guard was from Canada. I just loved this kid. She was a fun, hard-working, competitive fireball. She was hilarious, too; we enjoyed a lot of laughs together. I worked with her to help bridge the gap between the coaches and her. Sometimes the intensity was too much, but we'd find a way to ease that with some good laughter. She was a leader and the team loved her, so we needed her to keep a cool head. It was fun to help and support her as she found her way through the challenges and pressures of PAC-10 hoops.

At TCU, we were each assigned five players to meet with weekly. We were told to stay on top of their academics and make sure all was going well off the court. I had one player that was struggling academically, and I took it as a personal challenge to help her succeed. I decided the best way to figure out how to help her was to walk in her shoes. I would go to class with her to see how the teacher was presenting the material and take notes. Then she and I would compare notes after the class. I worked with her specifically to teach her how to take notes so that she could be successful in all her classes, not just this one. The strategy paid off, as she was able to successfully complete her degree and eligibility. That was a really rewarding experience as a coach.

At Iowa State, I had another "special project." This was a player I had recruited all the way from Ohio, and I felt personally responsible for her success. She was a great kid: fun, energetic, with a great sense of humor, but she had trouble focusing at times. She had the perfect game to fit into the Iowa State system. Of course, the baseline truth is that I don't like to be wrong, so I wanted to do everything in my power to prove that it was not a mistake on my part to recruit her. I was the guard coach, so I spent a lot of time with her on the sidelines. It was a challenge to keep her focused, but we worked through it. She only played a little bit her freshman year, but ended up being a very solid player for Bill Fennelly and company, so I consider that a personal victory.

Life and Death Is In Your Mouth

Words can hurt or heal. Whether you know it or believe it, everything that comes out of your mouth has an impact. This was a big revelation to me, and it was an important area of self-examination in my life. For example, I had to evaluate what kind of coach I had been:

- Am I a screamer?
- Am I an encourager?
- Do I only call out negative things?
- Do I use sarcasm?

What you say has the power to build someone up or tear someone down; there is no gray area. This hit me pretty hard as I started to take note of what came out of my mouth when I was coaching. I was a very intense coach. I expected a certain level of intensity from my players, and that was how I coached. I said my share of not-so-positive things, particularly after a loss. I would like to go back and have a "do over" with those teams. Unfortunately, I can't. However, I can change my words going forward, and try to help you think about these things so you can have a more positive impact on your team.

The NEGATIVE Coach

When I talk to coaches, or observe them on the court, I see a lot of negativity. I would say for every 10 negative comments I may see one positive comment. I had a coach tell me, "if I smile at this group they will just crumble." I find that hard to believe.

My personal development coach, Dani Johnson, does this exercise at business conferences. We get into groups of four (usually complete strangers) and each write down five things we admire about each of the other people in the group. Then we get to speak to each person the things we wrote down. It is such an awesome experience to be the giver of compliments (and then be the receiver of compliments). The feedback after the exercise is always amazing: everyone feels great, like they can accomplish just about anything they set out to do. I even do something similar in a quick little exercise with my teams: I put them in a circle and have them give one compliment to everyone on their right. Then we reverse and give a compliment to everyone on their left. It never fails—the giver and the receiver ALWAYS feel great after this exercise.

The power of a compliment is incredible.

Maybe this seems foreign to us as coaches because it is not the way we have been coached, or they believe that they are just doing what is expected of them. Why should I compliment them? My job is to point out what they are doing wrong so that they don't do it again. Yes, there is some truth in that. Our job is to coach, to teach, to correct, to train. You want to train the right habits, and correction is a necessary part of that process. But, don't forget to pepper in the compliments. If you see good behavior and recognize it, you will be sure to get more of the good behavior.

Have you ever heard the expression, "what you focus on you get more of?" Test it out, I dare you. Spend one day of practice only pointing out the positive behaviors. Track it and see what the results are. When negativity is poured out on people, it weighs them down. They can't possibly perform to the best of their ability.

I have been working on this at home with my own children. I went from being the mom that expected perfection out of my kids to a mom that offers more grace and forgiveness. Sure, we correct wrong behavior, but we emphasize affirmation and gratitude with our kids. Gratitude is done nightly and affirmation is emphasized on their birthdays...oh my! I just caught myself on this one. We need to fix that ratio.

The Sarcastic Coach

Another common coaching style I have seen and experienced is the sarcastic coach. Sarcastic humor mocks or ridicules, usually by saying the opposite of what is actually meant. I worked with a coach who used sarcasm as a coaching style (not one of the college coaches I worked with; it was with younger kids, so don't try to guess who it was). I found myself becoming very uncomfortable with his remarks. I didn't see good reactions out of the young girls we were coaching, either. It was a competitive group of girls, so they still worked hard, but I could see there was nothing positive coming from it. In fact, it created more confusion than anything else. There is really nothing good about the sarcastic approach. An occasional funny comment is not a problem, but if this is your style, it would be a good idea to work on emphasizing a more positive and direct approach with your team.

If you lead with a negative approach to coaching, work on cultivating the "sandwich method" into your coaching style: Positive, Constructive, Positive. For example: "Hey Suzy, I like your hustle, your close out on defense needs to be quicker, great job encouraging your teammates."

Three Core Values

I am going to share with you three core values that I have embraced in the years since then, each representing a fundamental change in my thinking. This has a daily impact on relationships and all that I do.

I learned them all from my coach and mentor, Dani Johnson:

1. Learn to love people in all that you do. Meet them where they are in life with compassion and understanding.
2. Learn more about people than you do about your product (whether that product is something you are marketing or your own expertise and capabilities) and you will be unusually successful.
3. Work harder on yourself than anything else. Stay in a constant mindset of personal development.

The Right Ratio

In coaching, your product is your team's productivity on the court: you are judged by what people see (wins vs. losses). But if you really want to be successful, game prep should be only about 10% of the time you spend coaching. The other 90% of your time should be spent grooming your team and recruiting future players. If you spend 90% of your time on game- planning and only 10% on knowing your players, you are spending your time in the wrong proportions.

Throughout my career as an Assistant Coach, even before I learned the importance of valuing people, I emphasized relationships with my team. I enjoyed working with the players and the time I spent getting to know them, on and off the court. After all, the pressure to win was not on my shoulders. My job was to do all that I could before the game started to get the team prepared. During the game, my job was to support the Head Coach and keep the players on task with their assignments.

The pressure of game day is on the Head Coach, because his or her name is in the record book. This is not to say that the Assistant Coaches don't care, but the Head Coach has a bit more ownership, as he is in control of the game once the ball goes for tip-off.

Once I got to Akron, I learned how different the Head Coach's world is from the Assistant Coaches. Moving up through the ranks and working for different staffs prepared me to know and prepare every aspect of the program. But that 18-inch move from the Assistant Coach's seat to the Head Coach's seat is a big move and requires more than just what you know about the Xs and Os of the game: it requires more skill with people than anything else. If you want to be the leader the team needs, you must work on your own personal development

First, especially your people skills.

Part of being successful with people is accepting the fact that not everyone is like you.

Thought Patterns That Kept Me Isolated

When I chose to go to school and play basketball at Case Western Reserve University, I knew I was getting into a program that needed a lot of help. Case was a Division III university playing in two different conferences at the same time: The North Coast Athletic Conference (NCAC) and the University Athletic Association (UAA), both of which had very strong teams, including several that made it to the NCAA tournament. One of these teams, Washington University in St. Louis, even had a National Championship under their belt, so the competition was very good. I knew we had an uphill climb in front of us.

I always entered games with the underdog mentality that we could turn things around if we just worked hard, and I set out to do my part. I was a basketball junkie, so I was going to do whatever was necessary, but it didn't take long to realize that very few of the women on that team shared my passion and drive.

In the past, I have made the mistake of thinking that all athletes are wired the same way: they always compete to win, they are always intense on the court, and always have the drive to be the best whatever it takes. To me, winning was EVERYTHING; I took it so personally, I thought everyone was that way—or at least, I expected them to be. They went to Case for a great education; basketball was secondary. That was a hard pill for me to swallow. Of course, while they were thriving in the classroom, I learned the hard way that the academics at Case were no joke.

I was a "gym rat" and spent my extra time alone in the gym, shooting, lifting, and working on my game. The gym had been my safe place since I was a child. I could shut out all the other crap that was going on in my life and shoot for hours. I was super-dedicated to my craft and expected others to be just as intense about basketball, but they were more focused on their academics and getting a job after college. I can't fault them for that. I'm sure it served them well. If I had allowed any other pursuit to get my attention, I probably would have done the same thing, but I was going to pursue coaching, so it made sense that my passion for the game superseded all other interests. It also meant that I was alone in my own world at times, sometimes angry at the other players.

When game time finally came, I could get on the court and do what I loved to do. We had a decent team that racked up more wins than the season before, but the losses took a toll on me. After each loss, I would ice my knees and go sit in the dark gym and sob. I felt so alone, like nobody else was feeling the pain of losing, because they did not take it as hard as I did. My heart flooded with self-righteous anger toward those who weren't grieving with me. I was so deeply caught up in my own selfish needs: it was all about ME. I could not see what was going on with anyone else around me, nor how my leadership was dissolving around me. Raging against the loss didn't make me a leader; it made me a loner.

Through all my years of playing and coaching, I really thought that everyone should feel the same way that I did about winning and, more importantly, hate losing as much as I did. I believed they should react the same way I did, and if they didn't, they surely didn't care as much as I did. I didn't realize that I had been pronouncing judgment against others who didn't see things the way I saw them, not accepting the differences in my teammates' values, nor (later on) those of my players. In choosing not to accept or respect them for who they are, I was setting myself up to receive rejection back from them. I was not acting from a place of humility nor being a leader. In fact, I was exhibiting a very low level of leadership. There was so much fundamentally wrong with my way of thinking.

The Wrong Avatar

As coaches, we develop an avatar of the ideal type of player we want in our programs. I was looking for players that were similar to me, so that I could relate to them. If I could surround myself with people who thought and felt like me, I reasoned, then we would surely be successful. Imagine a whole team with my work ethic and competitive spirit.

Are you throwing up yet? I am writing this so that someone can learn from my mistakes. You can guess how this turned out.

If I had to do it all over again—and trust me, I really wouldn't want to go back through that exhausting existence—I would do things very differently. I would work to put together a balanced team that had a few players from each of the different personality quadrants, each bringing different strengths and weaknesses to the table. We would work to figure out how we all complemented each other. We would embrace the differences and gifts each brings to the team and discover how we can succeed by working together. We would work harder on knowing and valuing who we are as individuals and as a team.

It took me a long time to understand the differences in how people approach competition and life in general. Of course, I knew that we are each wired differently, with different passions and desires, likes and dislikes, how we dress and act, but understanding that we did not approach things on the court the same way wasn't clear until I coached my own daughter's fifth-grade team. This may be obvious to you, but bear with me, because it might help someone who thinks like I used to think.

There were times when I would correct Molly in practice and hear her giggle. It would make me so mad that she was being disrespectful. I had never really experienced this with other kids I had coached, believe it or not. They probably figured out that this wouldn't go over well. It was all the more aggravating because she was my daughter; it set a bad example to the team. I didn't want to yell at her, especially not in front of her team, but I was so irritated. We had a "chat" when we got home.

As it turns out, she was not trying to be disrespectful, it was her way of handling the "embarrassment" of being corrected. Oh boy, I thought, if she is ever going to be an athlete, this is going to be a tough road for her. How could she ever make it if she didn't have my intensity and laughed when she was corrected by a coach? GASP!

But she wasn't the problem in this scenario, and there was nothing inherently wrong in the mechanism she had developed to cope with embarrassment. I just needed to understand it differently. Today, she is a great athlete and I appreciate what I have learned from her, especially how she taught me to communicate with her and kids like her. Her smile comes out in her joy of playing the game. Witnessing that NEVER gets old.

My other daughter, Finley is another story. She competes super-hard, but is a complete goofball in the huddle. She gets distracted more easily and really doesn't like the structure as much as she just likes to have fun playing. Timeouts are very hard for her to keep focus. She is very athletic and talented, with quickness and great instincts on the court, and has arms that go on for days. She is a play maker, mostly off the ball, but she can shoot well, too: a great all- around player. She can dominate in most defensive situations, but she has such a soft heart for people that she doesn't want to hurt someone's feelings on the court. When facing weaker opponents, she slows her game to allow them to stay competitive.

Here's an example: during a game, I noticed Finley playing really relaxed defense and letting this little guard get to the basket and shoot it every time she had the ball. There was no attempt made at guarding her. I called a timeout and asked her what was going on. Why was she letting that girl beat her every time?

She responded by telling me she felt bad for her because she had a hearing aid. She didn't want to make her feel worse by taking the ball from her. I had to share with her that on the court she was a basketball player. She wants to compete and be challenged. She wasn't looking for pity. She is an athlete out there, and would want to be treated the same as the other kids. She understood and responded well. Just one example of how I am slowly learning how to coach her without being too aggressive, to push her buttons without pushing her away from the game. So far it is working. I am trying not to over-coach her, but simply sharing with her how she could execute a new skill and letting her work on it on her own.

Neither daughter is a duplication of my fierce competitive spirit. A big part of my growth as a coach, a mother, and a useful human being was to embrace that. My daughters have taught me more about coaching with understanding and compassion than any coach I have ever worked for or with. They have taught me how to teach with less intensity, so as to not offend or scare off the young kids. As a result, I have been having much more success and more fun coaching them. I think they are enjoying it more, too.

Hiring The Right People Is Critical

It's not enough for a coach to assemble a team of players that gel well and complement each others' strengths and weaknesses; it is just as important to surround yourself with a team of coaches that can work together to bring the best out of that team. It's not as easy as you might think.

As a young coach in my first Head Coaching job, I wanted to surround myself with people with whom I already had a good relationship, so I hired friends that I had worked with or played for in the past. That seems obvious, right? There is a lot to be said for having people on your staff that know you well. It is all good when things are going well. The problem comes in when people on your staff don't see eye-to-eye. As the leader, it was my responsibility to manage my staff and keep everyone on the same page, but some things were just outside my ability to control.

What I learned from that experience is that we each have our own life baggage that we bring with us wherever we go, unless we learn to deal with it appropriately. Unfortunately, I learned this too late to salvage my opportunity there. My staff was not functioning well. There was so much tension, and I knew that I needed to make difficult and unpopular changes before the wheels came off the tricycle completely. My longtime friendship with each of these great people had gone from being an asset to a liability. Even though I had a working relationship with each of them, they didn't all necessarily see eye to eye. It created tension on the staff. I labored under the decisions to let people go, knowing the devastating effect it would have on any of them. I couldn't do it. I saw and felt the toxicity growing in the whole organization—it was killing us all bit-by-bit, but I feared the pain I knew my decisions would cause.

I take full responsibility that I didn't have the courage to make the changes that needed to be made. It ultimately led to me being let go, which also hurt the people that I tried desperately not to hurt. That is a tough one to swallow, for sure. It took me a long time to forgive myself for my weakness and lack of courage to do what needed to be done for the good of the whole team.

The recovery from that failure forced me to look back at the deep, silent wounds of my childhood. I noticed a parallel between this situation and my parents' relationship. Mom and Dad were toxic. Dad was abusive and needed to be kicked out of the house, while Mom needed to have the courage to step up for the rest of us. I am not blaming my Mom at all, even though it sounds like I am. I am simply drawing the parallel here. We live what we learn. Studies show that most abusive people were abused themselves. Most bullies were once bullied by someone else in their past. I mirrored the lack of courage that I observed as a child. The fear of confronting a problem head-on was deeply rooted in me, but I have since learned that it is possible to break that cycle.

That knowledge alone would have made me a much better coach. I likely wouldn't have made the poor decisions and mistakes that led to being fired—not as many of them, anyway. At the same time, you can make the case that I wouldn't have experienced the transformation that made this book possible. If I had known my God, my Heavenly Father, as a loving, compassionate, wise counselor, slow to anger, and a source of strength and guidance in all my difficulties, there wouldn't be a story to tell. I would have turned to Him long ago.

What I know now is that my story is already written. He knows every hair on my head. He loves me deeply and has a good plan for me. Jeremiah 29:11 says, "For I know the plans I have for you, declares the Lord, plans to prosper you and not to harm you, to give you a future and hope" (NIV). He wants good for me in my life. It will not come without struggles, but He is with me in all that I am doing. His hand was in everything I had done to that point, I just didn't know it. Had I known what I know now, I would have known that, "I have strength to do all, through Messiah (Jesus) who empowers me" (Philippians 4:13, The Scriptures 2009). I would have had the wisdom and strength to handle my staff and my team for the good of all. But that wasn't His story for me. I had to go through my struggles to get to where I am today. I now know that "all matters work together for good to those who love Elohim (God), to those who are called according to His purpose" (Romans 8:28 The Scriptures 2009). He has bigger plans for me.

A complete disclaimer here. I am not blaming my staff for my mistakes and poor leadership. The "buck stops here"! It was my responsibility as a leader to build a team in my staff to successfully lead our team of young women. I take full responsibility for my lack of leadership.

The Things That Really Matter

Think about this: if you knew that ALL things would work out for good if you loved God and followed Him, how would that change your life? What if you coached in the belief that God has it all written out already—every win, every loss, every injury, every recruit—and the plan is already set? Would you find peace in that? Now, don't get me wrong, that doesn't mean that you don't have to put in the work. God is not some genie in the sky that sits up there and nods His head to make magic happen. He COULD control every situation, but He doesn't. Humans have free will and that affects everything that happens in life. There are God-fearing people and there are non-believers, people who obey Him and people who don't, so stuff is going to hit the fan. But, KNOWING that He is there to work out every situation for good...how does that make you feel?

Think about it:

- Would you coach differently?
- Would you find more joy in what you do?
- Would you worry less?

Here is what the Bible says about worrying: "Do not be anxious about anything, but in everything, by prayer and petition, with thanksgiving, present your requests to God. And the peace of God, which transcends all understanding, will guard your hearts and your minds in Christ Jesus" (Philippians 4:6-7). Imagine feeling the PEACE that surpasses all understanding. If you work with diligence and excellence as He calls us to, and rely on Him in your weakness, you will be amazed at what this will do for you. This is the heart and soul of my message in this book.

I was that coach that worked my tail off, watching game film at 2:00 am while trying to nurse my daughter and wondering why she couldn't settle down. Yielding to the all-consuming pressure of having to do more, more, more. I would outwork my opponent in game preparation, thinking that would get the job done, when in reality, I needed to spend more time working on my relationships than anything else:

- My husband, who walked alongside me through all of this. How could I have survived any of this without his stabilizing presence in my life, even when I wanted to punch him sometimes...or more likely, him wanting to punch me.
- My girls. Teams come and teams go, but these girls

are my legacy, the fruit that will really matter when all is tallied up at the end. When I hang up my whistle for the last time, will they still be there to call me "Mom"? Only if I manage these relationships right.
- The relationships with my players. The X's and O's are important, but spend more time studying and learning your players than you do on game film and you will know how to draw the best out of them and enjoy greater success. In coaching, success from the outside world is measured in the win column, but coaches know there is so much more that goes into what we do. The true success is seeing them develop as incredible young women when they graduate.

But above all of this, the one relationship that matters most is my relationship with my Heavenly Father, my Papa, who loved me more than I could love my own children. If you question that, think about this: pick one of your children (if you don't have children then pick one of your players) to give their life to save your family, your team, whatever you think is important. God gave His ONLY Son—His own flesh and blood—to die a brutal, painful death for YOU. I am sorry, but I could not imagine volunteering one of my children to go through that suffering. No way! That is the most unselfish love anyone could ever lavish on us, and your Heavenly Father did it for you. Isn't that a relationship worth cultivating?

One hundred percent of the criticism we receive is from the 10% of our time that we spend on the court, and as a coach it is hard to separate from that outside critique, but I have learned to live my life for an "audience of ONE." Yep, you guessed it: my God is the ONE. Colossians 3:17 says, "And whatever you do, in word or deed, do everything in the name of the Lord Jesus, giving thanks to God the Father through him." First Corinthians 10:31 says, "So, whether you eat or drink, or whatever you do, do all to the glory of God." It is not easy, but I know that I continually have to work at keeping God as the center of my life.

As I look back, I can see that I made basketball my "god" for most of my adult life. After all, I found my identity in being a basketball coach. That is why getting fired from that all-important coaching job was so traumatic for me. I lost my identity when I ceased being a coach. Life revolved around MY job. I would have never left coaching Division I college basketball if I hadn't been forced out of my job. That is 100% ego driven.

As it turns out, God had a plan for my life beyond coaching college basketball. It was the best thing that ever happened to me, whether I saw it at the time or not. God's hand was in this for sure. If I knew then what I know now, I would have accepted the job change and not allowed it to destroy my whole being. I would not have identified my whole self in basketball. I would have known that there was more to me, and that coaching basketball was something I did, not something I was.

Chew on that for a bit.

Is your entire identity centered around being a "coach," or is coaching something you do?

See Yourself

When I was helping athletes navigate the recruiting process, I would advise them to visit several campuses several times each, meet the coaches, and ask lots of questions. I even gave them a list of questions to ask. But the most important thing I would tell them is, "when you get on campus, picture yourself simply as a student. If a career ending injury took the opportunity to play basketball away from you, could you see yourself fitting in there?" The key was to help them cultivate an identity in something other than just basketball. Athletes play basketball; they are not "basketball players." They have more to their being than just their basketball abilities.

How strange it seems now that I never recognized my own struggle with identity.

I was able to guide my clients in how to approach recruiting, encouraging them to see themselves as more than a basketball player. Ironically, I did not see myself as more than a basketball coach.

As an Assistant Coach, I was very good at identifying with the athlete. I enjoyed the time I had to hang out with the players and get to know them, on and off the court. I was pretty good at relating to them beyond basketball. As I shifted to the Head Coach position, my focus on players gave way to the pressure to win. I began to focus so much more on strategies that I lost sight of the most important part of my job: the people.

My focus today in every opportunity I have to work with athletes is to see them as the amazing women they are designed to be well beyond their basketball abilities. And ultimately to help them see that identity in themselves. This is why I focus even more today on the people part of coaching than I do on the X's and O's. While it's true that I am coaching at a very different level, it is amazing to see how much better the kids respond as I have taken more interest in who they are over their basketball performance.

Stay Teachable

In my early days of coaching, I was a sponge. I made it my focus to take in everything I could to be a great coach. When my journey started with Southwestern's volleyball team, I was excited to learn and grow as a coach.

The game was faster, and the schemes much more advanced than at the high school level. I was fortunate to coach with Glada Munt, whose volleyball teams earned nine NAIA National Championship appearances and finished in the top 10 seven times, including a runner-up finish in 1981. She taught me a lot about volleyball and coaching young athletes.

I was also honored to work under Ronda Seagraves. Ronda had great success in NCAC at Allegheny College prior to coaching at Southwestern University. I only worked for her for one year, but learned a lot about the administration of a team as you wear many hats at the Division III level. At that time, it was rare to have a full-time Assistant Coach. I had the opportunity to get my feet wet in every aspect of running a program, including travel, player management, scouting reports, and recruiting. It was an awesome experience, and one to grow on.

Moving to Oregon was another step in my learning curve. There I was a full-time student and Assistant Coach. I had the pleasure of scheduling travel and handling a lot of the administrative aspects of the program. Jody depended on me to keep the office tasks running smoothly. There was no secretary strictly for basketball, so I had the opportunity to work directly with the athletic administration at the university for scheduling and planning. I took every opportunity to meet as many people in the department as possible and make a good impression. Remember, "you are on an interview every day of your life," and you never know where those relationships will lead. It also helped that my roommate, Allison, was the assistant to the Senior Women's Administrator. I got a lot of the ins and outs of the department from her.

I had the opportunity at Oregon to sit in on some meetings revolving about student-athletes and compliance as well. This helped to educate me on the academic and support services side of the business. I remember sitting in on a meeting that discussed whether athletes should get paid or not. In 1995, TV revenues for universities was not nearly what it was today. Coming from playing Division III, paying for school, and playing sports, my viewpoint was that the athletes are earning a full scholarship (in some of the sports) and that is pretty good compensation for playing the sport they love. Today, with TV revenues in the billions of dollars, I have a very different viewpoint. The athletes should get strong consideration of being paid. There is always growth, and the dynamics are constantly changing, encouraging the constant consideration of change.

Moving on to TCU, it was easy to stay teachable. I was young and full of energy, wanting to learn and be the best I could be. Mike was great to work with and we had a lot of fun. There was little pressure and the only direction to go was up. It was a program that had struggled in the past, so it created a tremendous opportunity to take the program to a higher level. We worked especially hard in recruiting to bring in great kids.

Working with Mike on the court was different from what I had experienced at Oregon. Of course, every staff is different in how they are set up and how they divide up coaching responsibilities. Mike was an "X's-and-O's" guy, so he had that covered; he didn't want help in that area at all. That, of course, affected my thinking as I moved forward to be a Head Coach: I assumed the Head Coach was supposed to handle all the game planning and the assistants just did the player personnel development. I still took it as an opportunity to learn and grow, so I took ownership in the athlete personnel side of coaching. I used my strengths in academics and relationships to help the players to be successful.

Advancing at the college level was like climbing a ladder: each position created opportunities to move up to the next rung. It never made sense to make a lateral move. My next stop, at Iowa State, was certainly a step up from TCU. The Cyclones had just come off an Elite Eight season after beating UCONN in the NCAA Tournament. I was moving into a great position as an assistant under Bill Fennelly, which was a big honor. There was also increased pressure to show what I could do as an assistant. The biggest job at this time was to recruit great future talent, to keep the train rolling forward. I was hired because they determined that I was "good" at what I did, but I had to prove it.

I had always told my players to stay teachable, but again, I had a hard time hearing my own advice. Instead, I began to feel like I needed to prove myself. If I showed any weakness—like not having all the answers—they wouldn't respect me. To be humble and teachable would have shown vulnerability: that I did not know everything about basketball. I could have sharpened my sword there, but fear kept me feeling like I had to pretend to be something I wasn't.

The basketball season culminated in the NCAA Final Four. The goal was to be playing there, but that was a tough road to get there. If you weren't playing, you were attending the WBCA Coaches Convention. There were clinics and meetings and awards ceremonies throughout the week leading up to the Championship game. There were many opportunities to learn and grow at the convention. As the years went by, I was actually chosen to lead some of the assistant coaches round table discussions. The various staffs I was on were also asked to present at the basketball clinics. As my experience evolved from the "student" to the "teacher", I began to lose my own desire to learn. That was a HUGE MISTAKE – ALWAYS STAY TEACHABLE.

I have found over the last several years, "the more you

know, the more you learn that you don't know". The more I dig into learning, the more I realize that I don't know. It has driven me now to be a perpetual student. I want to be the best that God has created me to be and to use my talents to the best of my ability. God loves when we work at the gifts he has given us.

The Parable of the Talents

I would like to encourage you to grab a Bible and read the "Parable of the Talents" in the book of Matthew (chapter 25, verses 14 through 30). Even if you are familiar with the story, it always helps to reread it. You are likely to come across something different each time you do.

This is a story of not settling for things as they are but to use what you have and develop it to the best of your ability. I have applied this to my life and it encourages me personally to stay teachable and to grow constantly. As a coach, when I read this story, I think of that gifted athlete I've had from time to time that takes her talent for granted and doesn't work at it. She is content with her success and coasts by doing the minimum. God does not like when we get content and choose not to work with excellence and diligence at the gifts He gave us, but He loves when we take what He has given us and grow and improve in order to use it for good.

To the one who dug deep and worked to double the talents he was given the Lord said, "Well done, good and trustworthy servant. You have been faithful with little; I will make your ruler over much" (Matthew 25:21). If you are anything like me, you jumped to the big things and over time neglected the little things. My struggles and shortcomings that led to getting let go at Akron were really a result of a lot of little things that piled up into one heaping mess. I had to take time during my hiatus to identify what that meant for me. Again, it was not fun, but remember that diamond: it takes work to bring out the beauty.

Since I wasn't coaching a team at the time, I started to identify in my home and family life where I could apply this principle. I started with the little— working on my relationships with my husband and kids, taking care of our home with more diligence. Each day I made a point of asking God where I could be "faithful with the little."

Be careful what you ask for!

I'm kidding. He is so good and faithful to help me. He began to reveal more and more to me. This did not happen overnight; it took time to get to know Him. It started by creating the daily routine of reading a devotional every morning. It took five to ten minutes a day. That fed a longing and desire to start my day with Him. If I skipped that part of my morning, I felt something missing in my day.

Getting into God's Word may be a totally new adventure for you. At first, it may feel weird, like getting on that wobbly bicycle for the first time. Each time you try, you get a little more confident and less wobbly. The more you practice, the more comfortable you get. Take your time. Your Heavenly Father is right there with you, holding the back of your seat to steady you as you go. Now it's time to use that discipline that you preach to your athletes. If you just do a little bit every day you form good habits.

This might be totally foreign to you, or you might be familiar with the terminology, but from a different perspective. You already know that how you choose to look at something makes all the difference in the world. As coaches, we know how to push our athletes in order to prepare them for the games ahead. We know that the pressure we put on them strengthens them to handle the competition.

God is doing the same thing with you and me.

So now, my friend, YOU can stand firm in the love and

blessings of being a child of the One True God; to boldly share this message of love with others.

When it's all said and done, the statistics will be forgotten, the record books will be rewritten, and the memories of the victories—and defeats—will fade. What matters most is what is etched in the minds of the lives that you impact by the influence you have on them.

If you have regrets, pray about them. Ask for forgiveness and know that no one is too far gone to be saved by Jesus. Then walk in the truth and freedom of knowing God, working to please Him and not those around you.

6
Coaching Is A Challenge At Every Level

IF YOU ARE READING this book, most likely you are a coach at some level. All of these classify as coach: mother, father, manager, teacher, CEO, etc.). What I have learned, first and foremost, is that God planted in you a desire to make a difference in others' lives through the gift of athletics.

- You are a leader.
- You are strong.
- You are courageous.
- You are bold.
- You are not afraid of a challenge.
- You love competition and want to use those gifts to inspire others.
- You want to influence young people beyond the boundaries of the court or field.

In this chapter, I will reflect on the challenges of each level and then share what I have learned through the years. Over the last 29 years, I have coached basketball in NCAA Division I, NCAA Division III, AAU, Recreational Sports and

Individual Instruction, High School softball and tennis and NCAA Division III volleyball. Looking back on each of these stops in the journey has taught me a lot about the person I was and the person I am today. Thank God for his grace and mercy! I can truly say I am in the best place I can be today.

Hopefully, you will glean some nuggets of wisdom, through my successes and failures, that can help you to better navigate your journey and set a vision for future success.

I will take you through each level and share insights and stories that may help you to stretch beyond where you are today. After you finish reading and reflecting, I would sincerely welcome your insights and stories that may help me to make a bigger impact, as well. I am always learning and would love to hear from you.

Private Instruction

I love working with athletes who are passionate about improving their skills. To work with me one-on-one, you have to want to learn. I always tell the kids to be very thankful that their parents are making this kind of investment in their passion for the game.

I work with kids from age 9 (believe it or not) to high school kids preparing for college and I start out by learning about the athlete and his or her goals. Their goals are usually summed up in: improving shooting consistency, getting better at ball handling, making the "next" team. My goal for each and every athlete is to help them meet their goals of advancing to the next level, whatever they may be. But most importantly, helping them to believe in their own ability and develop confidence through improvement of skill development.

I am a teacher of the game; to teach is to instruct, educate, train, and discipline. Players I work with are going to get a lot more than to simply improve their basketball skills. My greatest teaching skills include:

- To improve efficiency in ball-handling skills
- To become quicker and more explosive by working on their actual dribbling technique
- To improve shooting consistency through mastering the form and footwork
- To become stronger mentally to handle the ups and downs of the game and to bounce back quickly after mistakes on the court
- To become the best teammate through a better understanding of themselves and the game

The first session is always assessing the skill and technique then sharing the plan to improve. The plan is different if it is in the middle of the season versus in the summer. Mid-season work would be geared to tweaking the present techniques, focusing on improving footwork and quickness. The summer may require shot reconstruction and more in depth reprogramming of muscle memory. If they are willing to put in the work we can fix just about anything.

I have had really good success with my players. Perhaps one of the greatest lessons I learned from the Bible is, "life and death is in the power of the tongue." Anything that comes out of my mouth has an effect on my athletes— either good or bad. I am very conscious of the words I speak and do not speak to my athletes.

I have a few favorite stories that show the depth of challenges a coach can face in private instruction:

Sandra

Sandra came to me during her junior year of high school. She was really struggling mentally with her high school coach. He played mental games with the kids and she just never knew where she stood: one game he would make her a starter and the next game he would give her three minutes of play time. She was a fierce competitor with a good shot. The problem was she was inconsistent, and a big contributor to that was lack of confidence. When coaches start to mess with kids' heads—like changing rosters without communicating and then pulling them for any mistake made—is a recipe for disaster, especially with a 16-year-old girl.

I had a blast working with Sandra. She was a bright girl with an energetic personality and great physical strength; plus, she was a natural leader with her teammates. She just wanted to get better to have a more positive impact on her team.

We spent an hour each week mid-season tweaking her shot and working on her footwork and ball skills. But the most important work we did was on her mind. We talked about the challenges she was having with the coach. I would work on building her up as we worked out with words she needed to hear and internalize: "you are strong, you have a strong shot, you are a winner, you play hard, your work ethic is beyond measure, your commitment to your team is amazing because you are here working." The more confident she became in herself and her own abilities, the more consistent her shot became. Coach recognized her improvement and she not only became a consistent contributor to her team, she ended up being one of the strongest players by the end of the season and had Division III coaches looking at her to play college ball. She ended up playing on the club team at Ohio State and having a blast for four years in college.

Tom

Tom was in seventh-grade, lanky and athletic with the quickest first step I have seen in a long time. Surprisingly, Tom did not make his seventh-grade basketball team. I was actually shocked after I saw him attack the rim. His shot needed work, but his explosiveness and ability to finish around the rim was incredible for a seventh-grader. When we began our workout, he was really tough on himself. Every missed shot he would throw a fit. Then, when I was working on shooting form, his frustration came through by whipping the ball back to me in anger.

AHA! I stopped the lesson right there. I told him, "not making your team has nothing to do with your ability but everything to do with your attitude. You are not being coachable and frankly, I don't think you want to be here."

"I do," he replied.

So I said, "OK, we have 20 minutes left in this workout. You need to show me you can be coachable." The last 20 minutes weren't rainbows and sunshine for sure, but we got through it.

I had a talk with his dad and told him my thoughts. I figured for sure we were done. Nope, the next week the dad called me again for a workout. I told my husband that this one was tough. Working with Tom was way beyond basketball and I wasn't sure I had the tools to work with him. I prayed about it for a bit. I figured there was a reason he walked into my life, so I needed to do what I could.

I am not going to lie, it was a battle. He had major anger and frustration issues. Every miss was the end of the world. I decided I needed to dig deeper into Tom. I started asking him some questions about what he did for fun, what subject he liked in school, and then what's your mom up to while you and your dad are at the gym.

"My mom died when I was 10." WHOA!! That was a shock.

"Oh man, I am so sorry to hear that. Was it cancer?" I asked. "No, she just didn't wake up one morning from bed." Holy smokes, that gave me some pretty good insights into Tom. He was struggling with some pretty heavy stuff and never really learned to handle it. I knew this because of all the self-reflection I had gone through myself over the past several years.

After further discussion with his dad, I learned that he was on medication and seeing a psychiatrist. Oh my, another issue I have never dealt with like this! He asked if I would be willing to talk to his psychiatrist and discuss how we could work together to help Tom.

She and I agreed: he needed to be held accountable for his actions to make changes in behavior. She was talking about it with him and I was actually implementing it with him on the court. It was a grind working with him most days. It took a lot out of me mentally every time we met in the gym. We stayed the course and he kept coming back.

I would love to say we turned this around within a year, but he did not make the eighth-grade team either. He played in after-school leagues and continued to work on his game. I would ask him every week if he started attacking the basket yet. I knew the skills he had. He began to focus on his attack and his game got better. I continued to see him occasionally, and even went to a game to watch him play, to get better insights into his court demeanor. We kept working.

Finally, he entered ninth grade and High School tryouts rolled around. That's when I got the best message I could receive: "Tom made the freshman team." That was a huge success story for him. I was so happy to be part of it.

Building Family Trust

As I am reflecting on the kids I have worked with I am humbled by the number of families that would entrust their kids to me. It truly is my favorite time. I love the one-on-one teaching and watching kids have the skills "click" for them and succeed.

Jake

Jake is the kindest kid from a great family. He was tall and strong and had a passion for basketball. He was super-smart, too. I love working with smart kids who are coachable. Those are the easy ones, for the most part. Jake had some good skills and good athleticism, but his biggest enemy was his own mind. The mental part of the game is so important with athletes, no matter what age. Remember, coaches, "life and death is in the power of the tongue."

Jake and I worked together on his shooting skills for two years and he developed a great shot. With his build, he was likely going to play inside, as well as out. So, we spent a lot of time working "back to the basket" skills too. We went through the baseline shooting series that I would do when I coached the posts at TCU. I really enjoyed working with the "bigs," helping them with footwork and scoring. Jake had great hands around the rim as well—he was a good finisher.

Jake's problem was he would get in the game and get sped up and not always finish. I taught him to go strong and get fouled. Earn your points at the line. It was two weeks before the high school tryouts. He was a freshman at a high school with great basketball tradition. I wasn't quite sure how he would fare. My advice to him was, "you don't need to be a scorer—there are enough guys who want to do that. What you need to do is be the best at doing the 'dirty work:' be the best rebounder and defender and get on every loose ball. Those are things the coach will notice because not everyone wants to do it. Trust me." Tryouts came around and he made the freshman team. A month into the season I saw his mom and she said, "he's not scoring, but he's on the court 75% of the game. It's because of you." I told her, "he's the one that did the work." I was super proud of Jake.

Individual workouts are an amazing way to help kids to reach their goals. Skill development is so important. Kids and parents often think that playing more games is what is important. They need to get in the gym on their own and work on the skills so that they actually get into the game, otherwise they'll spend all that game time on the bench.

Savannah

Savannah is a perfect example of using her time wisely to work on the skill development. Now, it is true that she is 6'2" with a great athletic build and can jump out of the gym. But her mom, who is a coach, did not allow her to play in exposure events that college coaches can view until after her freshman year of high school. Instead, she spent that time in the gym mastering her own skills. Rather than running up and down the court, getting 30-40 touches per game in the summer of her freshman year, she was getting hundreds of touches every day. As a result, after her first summer out on the recruiting circuit, she got offers from many big-time Division I basketball schools. Skill development is key to becoming a great basketball player, no matter your level of ability.

My Greatest Victory

I have experienced championships at the NCAA Division I level all the way down to the middle-school level and other great victories as a player and coach.

You're probably thinking I am going to tell you about one of the Big XII Championships or an amazing NCAA tournament win that advanced us to the Sweet 16. Or how about the 127-125 triple overtime victory over our cross town rival SMU at TCU. Although those were exciting and fun, they don't hold a candle to this victory.

It was the first playoff game for my seventh-grade team. I wasn't sure if we would even have five players for the game. Collectively, my five potential players missed 15 days of school the week prior due to illness—my daughter had missed four days. One of my players had a headache that morning. Her mom reached out to me. I said, if there were any way she can be there to start the game, we could go from there. We needed five girls to start the game, but we could end the game with four. She showed up, but really did not feel like playing. As far as I knew, we would end up playing with four.

The game started out rocky for us. We were down 9-2 at the end of the first quarter. That is when I challenged the girls: "I understand you all had a rough week, but you know how to play this game, and you are tough. We know how to play good defense, but we were just standing around in the first quarter, giving up layups. I know you have it in you."

As the second quarter started, we went down and buried a three, then got the ball back and buried another three. It was suddenly a 9-8 ball game. We scored 15 points in the second quarter and entered half-time tied at 17.

GAME ON!

My girls battled through the rest of the game, playing their hearts out. They really left it all on the court. At the end of the third quarter, we were down 27-26. "Keep on fighting, girls!" I cheered. "No matter what happens in this game, you are warriors!" I was so proud of their effort. We were still playing with five girls—no subs. They were exhausted but kept battling.

With 20 seconds to go in the fourth quarter, we were up by two points. All we needed to do was get a stop. We defended hard and got a tip on the ball, causing a loose ball. They recovered and made the shot as the buzzer sounded.

It was good. The game was tied 33-33, and we headed into overtime.

The first overtime rocked back and forth. With 15 seconds left in overtime and the score tied, Finley got fouled shooting a 3-pointer. I felt pretty good— she just had to sink one to ice it.

She missed all three! Double overtime!

The girls were exhausted and crestfallen, but they took a deep breath and soldiered on. A few minutes in, Finley got fouled, set up for her 1-1 shot, and drained them both. So, with a minute to go, we were up by two. Suddenly, Bella fouled out and we had to finish with four tired players. The girl who came to the game not feeling well battled through the whole game.

Four on five, we got the steal and Finley chucked it up the court to Maria. Maria turned, tossed it up, and drained it, leaving us up by four, with one minute to go, and four players. The girls ran out the clock to finish an epic battle.

I can only describe the sensation that pulsed through my veins as pure joy and pride for how these girls competed and battled through that game. I circled them up and told them it was the greatest display of courage and guts I had ever seen on the court. They showed incredible will to compete and finish. I felt myself get emotional, but Finley gave me that smile only a daughter can give and whispered, "Don't, Mom."

Too bad, kid. I couldn't help myself.

We did win the game, but that was not the best part. Afterward, the site administrator came over to me. She had been sitting at the scorer's table the whole game, and we'd had a couple of short interactions, but she had heard my talks with the team during timeouts. It was full-on transparency of all that I did during that intense game. She came over to me and said, "I am so impressed at how calm you were the whole game with your team. I admire that."

For me, those words were the greatest victory of my coaching career. It was evidence that I had grown and learned to control my emotions and behavior in a positive manner with my team. It was an intense game—there were times I could have really gotten after the officials, but I didn't. I could have gotten after my team, but I didn't. I learned so much about myself in that game. I can say that those words mean more to me than any championship. To top it off, in prayer that evening, as a family we go around and say what we are thankful for. Both Finley and Caitlin separately said how thankful they are to have their mom as their coach. I would say I have come a long way baby!

Youth Sports

We could talk about youth sports for hours. It has become a multi-billion-dollar business. Did you know that this is one of the few industries that does not suffer in a time of financial depression? People would rather go into debt than see their kids miss out on sports. This may explain some of the crazy parent behavior that we see at various events—not just on the travel-team circuit, but in the church leagues as well. The money that has been poured into the multi-billion-dollar collegiate sports industry has created a trickle- down into the youth organizations, creating the mindset that every kid can get a college scholarship if they focus on that sport and put everything they have into it. The truth of the matter is only 3% of high school athletes play at the collegiate level. Only a fraction of middle schoolers make the high school team. You do the math, it is a special kid that goes on to play in college.

Let's talk about travel sports for a minute. I am going to talk from the perspective of AAU (travel) basketball, because that is what I know best, but the principles hold true for all sports. Growing up playing AAU was not the norm. It was the elite kids, the standout kids, that played. There was the AAU Junior Olympics and that was about it.

Now fast-forward to when I was coaching and recruiting collegiately. Early on there were four or five huge tournaments that were sanctioned for recruiting. The best of the best were at those events. We spent about six weeks from late June to the beginning of August following the same kids and coaches from one event to the next. I always joked that the coaches could have saved a lot of money by simply chartering a flight together and going from location to location. It was exhausting, but I was young and enjoyed the camaraderie on the road.

As the years went on, the popularity of AAU exploded. Every parent could see their kid being the next Cheryl Swoops or Diana Taurasi. They just needed to make the AAU team. Well, program directors smelled money. If you could write a check, you could make an AAU team. These kids needed a place to play, so they created more tournaments for more teams, which totally watered down the competition. Now, every kid that wants to play, even if they are not skilled enough, can pay to play on a team. It is an interesting experience. My first year of coaching AAU was helping to coach my daughter, Finley's sixth-grade team. We just played in local events to get the girls some experience. The problem is the same six teams are playing in all the same tournaments, so you don't face different competition. There are a few good teams that challenge us and a few really bad teams that give no competition.

This brings up two important questions:

- Does playing bad competition do anything for the girls' development?
- Is playing a bunch of games all summer helping in their development?

Coaches would always say the real work is done in the summer. What they meant (before all these travel teams were a dime-a-dozen) was that summer was the time the kids got in the gym on their own and worked on skill development, developing better ball handling skills, working on shooting form and consistency, and getting up thousands of shots. You can't get better by shooting 10 shots a game or 30 shots in an AAU practice. The AAU coaches are more concerned with putting in plays than skill development.

This is why playing more is not always the answer. The true answer depends upon the goals of the athlete. If the player is simply enjoying running around with her friends and likes to play every weekend of the summer, then by all means, go play as much as you want. However, if the goal is to improve skill to be a competitive player and advance levels with the goal of playing in college, then more time needs to be spent in the gym on skill development, especially at the youth and middle school levels. Bad habits are formed in these games if the proper skill development is not being done. Don't fall into the trap of "more is better." More skill development, YES; more games...not necessarily.

I've also noticed that parents give the kids too much say in what they want to do. Mary played for me in sixth-grade AAU. Mary really liked playing for me. She really felt she was learning a lot about the game of basketball. Although we had limited time in practice, I always made sure to teach the fundamentals, especially how to play great team defense. I also taught offensive techniques and movement at a higher level than most AAU coaches.

As I was working out what to do for the coming summer for AAU, her dad sent me a message to explain his dilemma: Mary really likes playing for me and knows she will learn a lot, but she saw her friends who played for this other AAU program playing well into June and had more games, and she felt like she was missing out. FOMO was setting in. So, I sent my thoughts to her dad.

Dear John,

Thank you for reaching out to me about Mary. I am so happy to hear that she enjoyed playing for me. I really enjoyed coaching her as well. She is a great kid with lots of basketball potential. She has a good understanding of the game, plays hard and has a foundation of good skills. Regarding your dilemma of where to play this summer, it is important to consider her age and long- term goals. At the middle school level they are sponges and learn at a rapid pace. The basketball knowledge that she will gain with our team is likely more than she will get with the other program. You have seen how I work with the kids and teach the fundamentals. With the other program, she will certainly play more games. It seems to be a question of quality over quantity. My philosophy at this age is to get them experience playing against the better competition without overdoing it. More is not necessarily better. Mary should spend time in skill development and working on mastering her shot and ball skills. In addition, you said she wants to play club volleyball at the same time. Please be aware of the potential for overuse injuries, very common at this age as the kids are growing. I understand this is what Mary wants, but I caution you on that decision.

Sincerely,
Kelly

I saw John at our club volleyball fundraiser. Mary was playing club volleyball and did go with the other team. Her mom said, "we are letting her direct us on what she wants to do." Parents, please be the parent. Kids make decisions based on emotions. They are not equipped to make the decisions that truly affect their development. Be the parent, not the friend.

Recreational Sports

There is another sector of youth sports that we may all be more familiar with, Recreational Sports. Rec sports are to give every kid an opportunity to play. To experience the fun of competition and spend time with their friends doing what they love to do. The kids all know this but it is really amazing how the coaches and parents seem to forget this.

My Rec ball experience growing up and now coaching is in the CYO (Catholic Youth Organization). The mission of CYO is "to know God, to love God and to Serve God through athletics." The idea is that no child is left behind. There are no cuts and there are minimum participation requirements for the games. There is also mandatory coaches' training and coaches need certification to coach. The coaches we get in CYO are strictly volunteers and 95% of the time parents of the athletes. This is a completely different coaching experience from AAU. The biggest difference is that, as a CYO coach you don't get to pick your teams (there are no cuts). Equal opportunity is given to the player that has walked into the gym for the very first time in seventh-grade and to the player who has played for four years, including AAU. That is a great coaching challenge.

I went from coaching at the highest level of collegiate basketball for 13 years to coaching youth sports. I often get the question, "how do you make that adjustment when you have coached at such a high level?" It has honestly been quite a process of learning and humility for me. I have had to learn through trial and error and frustration at times, as well. There is a lot more to coaching youth sports than you might think. I learned the hard way and will share with you what happened in the process.

When I started out coaching my oldest daughter, Molly's team, I had the mindset that "everyone wants me to coach them, they are lucky to have my experience." That is such an ego thing that I am embarrassed to admit it. But that is why I am sharing this, so that you can learn from my "junk." I had the belief when Molly was in third grade (she is in high school now) that every little girl that played a sport had dreams of playing in high school (at least) and maybe even at a higher level. I am a sports junkie and thought everyone was the same.

Molly's group was quite an athletic little bunch of girls. We had 20 girls playing basketball in their grade, and most of them played multiple sports. They were really into athletics and the parents were gung-ho as well. I coached those girls with intensity, teaching them everything about the game. We ran a motion offense with movement and cutting, teaching them all the nuances of setting up the defender to make the back cut and delivering the perfect pass. On the defensive end, we had to run man-to-man until sixth-grade. We ran the shell drill, jumping to the ball, bumping cutters, working the head whip on the cut. These girls were amazing; they did what they were asked to do. We won every tournament we entered with these girls. It was certainly a lot of fun winning.

By the time sixth-grade came around, the teams we were playing had so much more size than we did. The parents all started to wonder if we were feeding our kids the wrong things, as our competition was always huge. So, to me, the solution was simple, teach them the match-up zone that we played at Iowa State. Now, I had some assistants (dads) that were very into grooming these little champions, too. We would work our defense 7-on-5 and the girls really caught on. I was loving it, my intensity grew as we got better and better. I wanted these girls to win because to me, winning was the most fun part of competing.

The key word there is "me."

I thought that every little girl was just like me and wanted to win more than anything. Because the girls were in sixth-grade, we could have an "A team" and put all the best kids on one team. This was going to be so great, I thought. I get to take the top kids and REALLY groom them for the next level. Practices were run with intensity and pace, because that is what you do to become really good. That's what ALL the girls wanted, right?

After an intense practice one night, I was in Molly's room tucking her in. She was very quiet and not saying much. I asked her what was going on. "Talk to me. You are in a safe place. What's wrong? You can tell me anything."

Finally, she cracked: "Mom, you're too intense."

Whew, that hit me and brought me to tears. I felt horrible as the last thing I wanted to do was to hurt my own daughter. This really hit me like a ton of bricks dropped on my head from the top of the Empire State Building. My poor kid was having to deal with her mom as the coach, and my expectations and intensity. That was a huge turning point in my youth coaching experience. I was going to be doing this for a long time yet. I had a second-grader and a fourth-grader that I was coaching at the same time. Lucky them, right? It really made me step back and reflect on who and what this was all for.

The Catholic Youth Organization (CYO) is really a phenomenal program. I grew up playing in it all through grade school; it was really the only show in town back then. Now, it is more of an opportunity to give EVERY kid an opportunity to be physically active and compete, no matter what abilities they have. I sensed that, if I was going to be coaching in this league for a long time to come, I had better figure out what that really meant. I started to listen at CYO meetings with a different ear and see through a clearer lens. I was fogged by my own competitiveness that I thought everyone shared. My job as coach was to teach kids how to compete with a "Jesus-like" vision. Whew, I was going to have to do more work on this area of my life; you can't teach it if you don't live it.

CYO always prays before and after games. The coaches are encouraged to pray at practice with the kids. I bought a little devotional book and began to use it at practices. Sharing a quick devotional and then applying it to sports. The girls liked it and called it "story time." I would use it before games as well. We had a great season their sixth-grade year and won the championship again, this time with a much better feeling about the journey and the outcome.

Seventh grade rolled around, and while the girls started to wane their interest in basketball, they still joined the program. What you may not understand, and I sure didn't at the time, is that between sixth and seventh grades, kids go through a lot of physical and emotional changes. They are starting to discover more about themselves and the social part of life becomes way more important than anything else. Their overall interest in basketball and competing did not match mine. I looked forward to a great, competitive season once again with this bunch. There was something missing. I just said how important this social part is, right? Well, I had missed that boat as I didn't take the time to get to know these girls when I was coaching them. I knew them as athletes and personalities, but I didn't REALLY know them as people.

It didn't help that I was coaching three basketball teams at the same time, either. I had Caitlin's third grade team, Finley's fifth grade team, and Molly's seventh-grade team. I was running like crazy in other areas of my life, too. We had 75 minutes to practice and get ready for this "A" team competition, so we had to get down to business.

Needless to say, the seventh-grade year didn't go so well. There were a couple of girls that I thought really had high school potential, so I would correct them more. Anybody who has EVER coached a day in their life knows that the better players get more attention, positive or constructive. Seventh-grade girls see that as being "picked on" and you don't like them because you are coaching them. A seventh-grade girl hearing her name called in practice with correction following does not see the positives in the situation.

I was encouraged by the "dad assistants" to give the girls a fresh voice to listen to. So, during their eighth-grade year, I stepped back and found a non- parent coach to finish out the year with them. It stung a bit and took a lot of humility on my part to let those kids go, but it turned out to be OK. While Molly was on the team, she was more into club volleyball. I was coaching Finley and Caitlin's teams as well, in addition to being the basketball commissioner organizing the program of 30 teams, so it really ended up being a blessing.

I took that time to make some changes in how I coached the younger girls' teams. The lens from which I viewed the girls' sports participation was becoming clearer, as well, which enabled me to be a better coach for my younger girls' teams.

Or so I thought.

That same year, I had Finley in sixth grade and Caitlin in fourth grade. Caitlin's group was pretty easy: I had a much looser approach with her at age 10 then I did with Molly at age 10. In my defense, Molly is our first, and I think most parents would agree that there is a huge learning curve with the first born. Caitlin is also wired differently from Molly. This is where I started to get a much better insight into my daughters' differing personalities. Caitlin likes to be silly and have fun; she likes to be the "class clown" and would do anything for a laugh. That's always tough when it's the coach's kid. I would have to reign her in to stay focused and quit screwing around. In order to help me with the relationship part of coaching the girls, I found a mom assistant rather than a dad. Moms just have a better way of looking at how girls react with each other and providing insights. This has been a great decision for me to keep me on task with the girls.

Finley's group added a different set of challenges. There were 16 girls out for the sixth-grade teams. We had to decide to make an "A team and B team" or to make two "B teams." Since I did an A team with Molly's sixth-grade team and it turned out well for us, I decided to do the A and B teams. I took the most athletic eight girls that had the best basketball potential of the group (key words: of the group) and made them the A team.

The basketball IQ of this group wasn't close to that of Molly's group. In fact, it was amazing how different they were. With this group, I tried my best to teach basketball, but I was the one that learned a lesson. Just because these girls are playing basketball doesn't mean that they all want to "learn basketball." I found that basketball was really just a means of social gathering for these girls, with a ball and hoops mixed in there, so the year was a grind. We played far better teams that actually had an interest in basketball, so we tended to come up short. Asking these girls to be competitive was difficult, since basketball was not their top reason for being out there. The year didn't end well for any of us, with a lot of frustration on both sides. There is much about that season I wish I could do over. From the mistakes I made, I learned it is best to step up and own up to your mistakes, apologize, and ask forgiveness.

I started a group at St. Hilary that I called Champion Athletes for Christ. It is similar to Fellowship of Christian Athletes (FCA). I met with sixth-, seventh-, and eighth-graders to talk about sports and God—specifically, how we can use our sports experiences to honor God. Many of my sixth-grade players were part of the group. I would use our own struggles and frustrations to model what it means to be a Christian in sports. Most importantly, we were able to share our frustrations in that group, and I was personally able to apologize and ask forgiveness for the frustrations I felt as a coach. It has really been awesome.

Now, I am coaching them as seventh graders with a much better understanding of who they are and their basketball expectations. We set up two B teams and played more fitting competitions, focused on the fun first, and then mixing in the basketball. It is amazing how much they are learning and the improvements they have made this season. I thank God for continuing to humble me to do His work through sports.

Though it is a "Christianity-based" league, there are many coaches who just don't get what we are doing here. No judgment (well, OK...maybe a little). I was coaching a game the other day, filling in for another coach, and using three of his players and two of mine to play his game. The other Athletic Director contacted me to please find a way to play the game because their girls REALLY wanted to play. I was already coaching 2 other games that day and did not want to do it, but I didn't want to let the girls on the other team down. So instead of forfeiting, we played the game.

At game time, one of the girls wasn't there: she had mixed up the start time and was on her way. So, I started the game with four players. The other coach really wanted to start before our other player arrived, so we did. After their first bucket, they put on a full court press. Wow, a full-court press with five against four, which was really unfair....in a Christian league! I was floored (My husband tells me I really shouldn't be surprised. REALLY.) I was not only surprised, but so disappointed in the behavior of the coaches. We were outmatched in the game, as two of our players had never played before that year. It was not a whole lot of fun to coach. To top it off one of my girls got injured, leaving us with only four players again. Even though they were up by 12 points, they put the press on again. This time, I yelled across the scorer's table, "are you REALLY going to press us with four players again?" "Oh gosh, we didn't know," the coach responded, trying to play innocent.

Did I mention that I am also the Athletic Director at our school? My job is to oversee our coaches, and this behavior really made me mad. After shaking hands, I called the coaches out about starting the game in a full court press against four players. The Head Coach gave me a shocked look and said, "what were we supposed to do, change our game-plan?" The answer is an unequivocal YES! This is called sportsmanship. The better solution at the beginning of the game would have been to start with four players until my fifth got there. That is surely what I would have done in that situation. To me, if you are going to compete, then compete fairly. If it is not done fairly, then it is not worth it.

The next week, I saw on the schedule that I would be facing that same team with my normal crew. I will admit, I went into that game with a burr in my saddle. (I knew about these from my Texas days) I wanted to prove to them that I knew how to coach with the kids I have been working with. I had "payback" in mind: don't mess with me (I know, that's really Christian-like). The day before the game, we spent the whole practice working on a press-break and a press, because we were going to beat them at their own game. I had my girls fired up to come out with all guns firing (do you like all those cowboy references?).

Game day arrived and we were ready to go. The ball went up and we were off to the races. They couldn't score so they couldn't press and turns out we didn't need to. We outscored them 20-4 in the first quarter. Our half-court man defense was more than they could handle. We worked the rest of the game on our motion offense, passing and cutting, making five passes before shooting, and could only attempt lay-ups. I sat my better kids as much as possible.

Later, I had to reflect on the emotions I had allowed to fire me up before the game. I was thinking about "pay-backs." In case you hadn't guessed, that is not a good way of thinking and coaching youth sports. I addressed it with the team and commended them for playing a very good, sportsmanlike game. They were really awesome.

The Purpose of Youth Sports

So, what is the purpose of youth sports? And why do kids play? As a coach and a very competitive athlete, I have to admit that, for years I thought all the kids played for the same reason I did: because they love competition and want to win. I learned so much by coaching my daughters from age five in munchkin basketball through middle school. One important thing I learned was that the number one reason that kids play a sport is to have fun. This one has always been a struggle for me. To me, fun was competing and the most fun was winning. That is where I had to do a mirror check... AGAIN!

In the summer of 2019, I had the opportunity to go through the "Play Like a Champion Today" (PLACT) training at the University of Notre Dame. They use research developed by coaches, professors, philosophers, sports scientists, theologians, faculty, and administrators from the University of Notre Dame and the Shaw Center for Children and Families, which is on campus. The focus of the program is:

- Put the child first
- Make sports about PLAY and fun
- Use sports to develop Champions in life
- Give your best
- Develop character
- Exemplify the characteristics of a Champion

It is truly a great program that helps coaches and parents to remember that kids are kids and they play sports for fun. Here are a few things that really stuck out to me in this research. They surveyed a large group of kids, "why do you play sports?" Take a look at the differences (and similarities) between the genders in the responses.

Boys

1. Have fun
2. Improve skills
3. Excitement of competition
4. Do something I'm good at
5. Stay in shape
6. Enjoy the challenge
7. Be part of a team

Girls

1. Have fun
2. Stay in shape
3. Get exercise
4. Improve skills
5. Do something I'm good at
6. Be part of a team
7. Excitement of competition

The NUMBER ONE REASON for both boys and girls: TO HAVE FUN

What I Learned at Notre Dame

As a coach, this is very important to keep in the forefront of your mind. I'll be honest: it's not easy for me. I am not naturally a "fun" coach, so I have to work at it. I have to step back regularly and examine what I am doing, to make sure I keep it fun.

The PLACT research recommended giving the kids input in practice, like choosing what drills they want to do. Ask them to identify what they think they need to work on and then set the plan according to their responses. This certainly takes more work, because you have to maintain a flexible practice plan, but it is worth it.

Another great component of the PLACT training is the GROW Approach. Their research has shown that this is the most effective formula to develop high performance athletes and athletes of character: Goals + Relationships + Ownership = Winning.

Goals

Parents and coaches should help kids to set physical, mental, and sportsmanship goals before the season, and then help them to reach those goals through encouragement and positive feedback. Be sure that the goals are personal and do not have to do with comparison to others on the team. For example, "Johnny wants to learn to dribble as well as Tommy" would not be a good goal because it is focused on comparison.

Relationships

"Building relationships increases team stability, cohesion, performance and player satisfaction." There are many relationships in basketball: player-to- player, player-to-coach, coach-to-parent, player-to-referee, coach-to-referee. Modeling how to create relationships through communication and example is a very important part of athlete development.

Ownership

"Champions take ownership of their games and lead responsibly." As parents and spectators, we are guests at our children's games. It is their stage; they put in the time and effort in practice, working with the coach to perform better in competition. Would you go to your child's dance recital and yell, "spin faster, jump higher?" I'm pretty sure you wouldn't. Keep that perspective at their sporting event. It is their game. Let it belong to them.

Winning

Can you be a Champion without winning the game? In reality, 50% of the teams in every game win and 50% lose. If you can focus on the principles of the GRO the W will take care of itself. It may not always end the way you want on the scoreboard, but they will learn to win in the game of life.

Long-Term Athlete Development

Another great message I took from PLACT is the Long-Term Athlete Development model developed by Istvan Bali. This model has become accepted worldwide. The model examines "early specialization" vs. "late specialization" of athletes.

- Stage 1: The FUNdamental Stage (males and females ages 6-10)
- Stage 2: The Training to Train Stage (males 10-14 years and females 10-13 years)
- Stage 3: The Training to Compete Stage (males 14-18 years and females 13-17 years)
- Stage 4: The Training to Win Stage (males 18 years and older and females 17 years and older).

This was particularly interesting to me I don't know if you've noticed this, but there is a growing trend of kids that are specializing in a single sport at an early age. The thought process of the parents (or whoever is influencing the decision) seems to be this: if kids specialize early in a sport, they are more likely to develop into elite athletes. Studies show early specialization can be beneficial for individual sports (e.g., gymnastics, figure skating, tennis, and so on) but for team sports, the focus should be on developmental training. Athletes who skip steps 1 and 2 seldom reach their full potential. You can't skip player development in the pursuit of the lofty goals. You will never realize those goals without working on the fundamentals and training.

If we are coaching for the right reasons, our focus in working with athletes should be the development of the overall person, no matter their age. In the youth arena, it is especially important to use positive, affirming words to nurture the growth of the athlete. It helps the kids want to continue participating in sports, it is a huge contributor in developing confidence and self-esteem, as well as developing a love for physical activity. Keep it fun and interesting for the kids and they will keep coming back. Go back to the list of reasons boys and girls play sports. Notice that "to win" didn't make either list. Kids don't come back each year because they won a championship; they come back because they liked the experience and it was fun for them.

High School Coaching

Coaching at the high school level is definitely different from coaching at the youth level. According to the Long-Term Athlete Development model, as we step up to high school, we move into the "training to compete stage." The athletes are in a deeper stage of mental and emotional development, so they can handle more complex strategic coaching. However, the high school scene is a total bump up for them socially and emotionally as well. There are the raging hormones and the newness of the high school environment, with increased responsibilities and heightened academic stressors as well. Oh yeah, and the fact that those who dominated in the youth leagues were now joining a team of those kids just like them. That certainly adds to the dynamics; managing bruised egos.

My own high school coaching experience will not help to teach you very much but I will share with you a little bit just to round out the story. I was just a 20-year-old kid myself when I started coaching. My high school coach was the Athletic Director at the time. She was in a pinch and knew I wanted to go into coaching. She gave me the nod.

My first charge was as the Head Tennis Coach. How hard could it be? After all, tennis was an individual sport and all the girls seemed to have their own trainers that coached them, anyway. So my brother, Keith and I took over the reins. Truth be told, neither of us had officially played tennis, but our dad would take us to the tennis courts as kids in hopes of grooming the next Chris Evert-Lloyd or Jimmy Connors. Keith and I had a lot of fun working together, but learned that tennis is a different beast than the team sports we had grown up playing. Let's just say we chalked that one up as an "experience."

In the spring, Kirbs, the AD, needed a JV Softball Coach. She was the Varsity Softball Coach I had played under for four years. This was a little more in my wheelhouse. Since my wingman, Keith, entered the real world of working, I took this one on my own.

As I said, I was practically a kid myself. I was a junior in college. I would park my car in the coaches' parking lot by the gym at Case Western, ride my bike to my classes, then zoom back to throw my bike in the car and get to practice. I would do anything to get my coaching career started.

How did I get to park in the "coaches" lot without getting tickets? NUGGET COMING : Make friends with the security guards who write the tickets. They were all my buds.

As I mentioned, being so young, the best thing I could do was to manage the game, do the lineup card, get the girls organized, and pray that we could hit the ball that day. I was super-competitive, and working with high school freshman and sophomores was not my strength at the time. I had already shared with you my thoughts on how I thought every athlete should have the drive and desire to win that I did. That certainly increased the challenge for me. Driving the girls in the school van to practice fields every day was a bigger challenge than the coaching itself. They were way more concerned with how their ponytails would look under their hat than they were about digging in and getting dirt on their pants as they hustled around the bases. I learned that I had a lot to learn about coaching a team and was pretty sure then that coaching at the high school level was not going the be the best long-term fit for me.

Since my high school coaching experience is not of most value, a better perspective will come from my experience working with high school athletes and parents on a more personal level. Thirteen years as a college coach and then 10 years assisting families in the recruiting process have given me a great deal of perspective on the high school student-athlete experience. In addition, I have had dozens of athletes that I have worked with individually in player development. This has afforded me opportunity to look through the lens of the athlete and the parents from many perspectives. But perhaps the most beneficial perspective is my own personal experiences as a parent on the sidelines of high school sports.

The Parental Perspective

This is by far the toughest role I have had to play yet: watching coaches manage their programs and seeing how it affects your daughter and her team.

Molly was just 14 and playing on her first high-school-level travel volleyball team. In the JO volleyball world it is called a "National Team." Obviously, it is an honor for a kid to get picked to play on the highest-level team, plus the coach had high accolades as a high school coach: he had teams play in state tournaments and may have even won a state championship. That was impressive and exciting. We figured we had a really good coach going into the season.

As the season pressed on, it was evident that the coach knew volleyball, but what he was lacking was the ability to groom this young team.

The team was made up of a bunch of 14-year-olds who:

1. Had not played together.
2. Had not faced this type of intense competition week after week.

The coach would get extremely frustrated when the girls were not winning. He would sit down and quit coaching. As a result, when his team was challenged, what do you think they did? Yep, they shut down and didn't respond well to the blows they were taking on the court.

There is way more to coaching girls than simply teaching them the fundamentals and tactics of the game. They need to be taught how to work together to bounce back from adversity. The resilience of the coach is always reflected in the resilience of the team, especially when they are new to a higher level of competition. It is so important for the coach to repeatedly instill in the team the fact that they will mess up, make mistakes on the court, fall down, and find new ways to fail. That is a given, but what do you do when it happens? The coach needs to teach them how to get up and move forward as a team—to fight through the adversity and rise above it. There are athletes that have those skills already, but the team needs to be groomed to do this and to rise up together. That is what a good coach does: he coaches through the tough times to help the athletes rise above adversity, even when the scoreboard doesn't show it.

Just Kids

In my recruiting business I had the opportunity to work with many young athletes that aspired to play college athletics. The goal was to help them find a college program that was a good fit. What I learned about these very good athletes is High School athletes are fragile—boys and girls alike. Even the most aggressive competitors are still "just kids" on the inside. They can put on a "bulletproof" front, but the truth is they live in a near-constant state of self- doubt, wondering what others are thinking about them, trying to measure up to one standard or another. I know that I have been guilty of not considering their fragile state of mind when I have been in "game mode." We tend to see "tough-as-nails" competitors on the court, and assume that we can "will them" to step up and handle big game situations as we continue to groom them for execution of the game plan, but the truth is, they are kids doing their best to please the coach and perform to the best of their abilities.

I went to a JV volleyball match this spring, and kept a close eye on the coach's reactions, and how they dealt with their players. Now, keep in mind, this was a JV game. I had been paying particular attention to the opposing coach. The ball was set to the Right Side Hitter, she was a bit out of position, plus it was not a great set. She was right-handed, but for some reason reacted and tried to hit the poor set with her left hand. As you can guess, it looked pretty awkward and ended in a side-out, careening off the net at her feet. The coach called a timeout and, as the girl was walking toward her, yelled at her (not her inside voice for sure), "What were you thinking?"

Well, coach, I thought I would swing with my offhand and look like a fool hitting the ball into the net...what do you think she was thinking, coach?!

She obviously was trying to make the best of a bad situation with less than one second of prep time and made a poor decision. I could almost feel that poor girl's heart breaking with embarrassment. I felt terrible for her.

As coaches and leaders, it is important to keep our cool and understand that these are kids out there trying their hardest to perform. I have never met a kid who is looking for an opportunity to screw up in front of their friends, family, and a bunch of strangers.

As I have spent more time over the years learning and growing and then observing the quality of some of the high school coaching, the thought of entering the High School arena entered my mind. I could surely put my "new and improved self" to good use on the bench.

This past year the Girls Basketball Head Coach position came open at my daughter's high school. I had several people tell me that I would be a great candidate for the position as it is a private, faith-based school. I gave it a lot of thought. I loved doing the individual workouts with the high school kids. And the thought that you can actually teach real basketball strategy and get into the nuances of the game with these kids was an intriguing thought. But then my husband woke me back to my senses. He got me thinking about what is involved in high school sports: the time-suck that it would be. In reality, coaching at the high school level is a full-time, 10-month job with very little pay. No, you can't do it for the money—the compensation could never make up for the time, blood, sweat and tears a high school coach puts in, not to mention the outside stressors of the recruiting that goes on now in high school.

I appreciate my husband's wisdom in shepherding me away from that choice.

The Biggest Challenge of All

Then, there is the biggest challenge of coaching high school sports: dealing with parents. I hear parents yelling at their kids when they make a mistake. Not just their own kid, but often the other kids, as well. The parent reactions when kids make mistakes is sometimes shocking to me. I often wonder how many of the parents played sports growing up; and if they did, to what extent? High School sports across the board have become more competitive since you and I were kids. More kids are playing sports and specializing early, so the competition to make the teams is (in most cases) much greater than we faced. It is often easier said than done to get out there and perform at a high level every night.

I have had the opportunity to coach and sit on the other side. I tend to have a much greater vision of the state of the program than most parents. That is not the case for most parents and so the disease of "tunnel vision" can be a big issue for coaches to handle. It is tough for some parents to see beyond their own child, with the constant focus on "how does this affect my kid" without the awareness of the big picture.

Our job as parents is to support our kids and let the coaches coach—even if we don't think the coaches know what they are doing. Yes, swallow your pride, as yucky as it tastes. The fact is, your kid is playing for that coach and needs to be on the same page with him. If you continue to muddy the waters, it will not end well for your athlete.

As parents, our job is to use every situation to teach our kids and prepare them for life's challenges. It is interesting, when you change your perspective, how difficult situations can benefit your child. We know as adults that we will not always see eye-to-eye with the leadership in our workplaces, churches, and other groups. Working with a difficult coach is an ideal, low-risk place to learn that. How an athlete responds to situations is a very good indicator of the advice they are getting at home.

You and I spend a couple hours a week watching our kids compete. The coaches are spending seven times that amount of time in practice every week, working with the team to prepare them for competition. As a parent myself, I am guilty of some uncomplimentary thoughts (I keep them to myself): I have been judgmental of coaches' decisions, but the truth is that we are not in practice and don't know what is going on behind the scenes within the team.

The job of a coach is HARD. Think about your job: what if you had bleachers in your boardroom at work, with people critiquing you and judging EVERY decision you make. You make the call to give Joe a raise because of his unseen contribution to reducing costs, and the crowd heckles:

"What the heck were you thinking? Joe is a bum. He doesn't deserve that. What are you? Crazy?"

Have you ever made an unpopular decision at work? Have you ever made a mistake in your job? How do you want your own boss to respond to you? Put the shoe on the other foot for a minute.

I've heard it said that what you focus on will flourish, and what you neglect will wither away. As parents, we can shape how our child will approach difficult situations. We can feed negative mindsets by telling them what we see the coach doing wrong, but this creates deeper roots of negativity and doubt in the coach, which spirals into more destruction, and can ultimately harm the athlete and the team. It also grooms them to be fired from one job after another for insubordination.

On the other hand, we can teach them how to use adversity to bring a team together. Teach them to be the voice of encouragement and positivity in the huddle and build the team up. Every team will face adversity, and every kid will have bad days and make mistakes. Teach them to get up and brush off the negative. Don't feed it, kill the negative immediately. Encourage them to be the light in the darkness they may be facing. This will serve them well in the BIG game, the GAME OF LIFE.

Coaching at the College Level

College coaching comes in many shapes and sizes. For those who are unaware, there are several different organizations that Universities fall under. Each has its own criteria for membership. Two of the largest are the National Association of Intercollegiate Athletics (NAIA) and the National Collegiate Athletic Association (NCAA), which is likely the most familiar. The NCAA has three levels: Division I, Division II and Division III. The most well-known being Division I, which hosts the all familiar NCAA March Madness basketball tournaments for men and women as well the the National Football Championship. Each organization has its own championships, but the DI matchups are the highly televised and most popular. The NAIA has two levels as well: Division I and Division II. The level within the various organizations has its own set of criteria for membership and a specific set of rules, most of which pertain to involvement of the student-athletes; including different scholarship allotments, recruiting calendars, and time commitment for the student-athlete. I have had the opportunity to coach at the NCAA Division I and Division III levels. My experience involving the NAIA is related to my involvement of helping athletes in the recruiting process.

In the interest of educating you, some of the other organizations are the National Christian College Athletic Association (NCCAA). A criteria for its membership is to be a

Christian-based college. The other is the National Junior College Athletic Association (NJCAA). These are two-year colleges that offer Associates Degrees. Junior College athletes can then be recruited to continue their playing career at a four-year university.

The college level is a whole new ballgame when it comes to coaching. Coaching in college is a full-time job. In my experience, it was not just a job, it was a lifestyle. Life revolved around the season and the recruiting calendar. Aside from managing your own team, recruiting is the biggest challenge that coaches face. At each level the recruiting involvement varied. The recruiting calendars set by the governing bodies of the organization set the rules for recruiting. The responsibilities of the coach are the same at every level.

Division III College Coaching

Just as I was the assistant for two sports, there are coaches that may have to coach an additional sport, be an assistant for another sport, or teach classes at the university, in addition to their primary role. Division III coaching salaries tend to be less abundant than salaries at the larger schools.

Of course, there are trade-offs to every situation: the external pressure to win is not as strong and the recruiting responsibilities are so much more limited than that of the Division I level. There is a price for everything.

Division III schools do not offer "athletic scholarships," although there are schools that seem to find additional financial aid for good athletes. I'm not sure how that works, but it has been done. The schools are typically smaller, private institutions with strong academic program. Since they do not offer athletic scholarships, the aid is based upon academic scholarships and financial need. This makes recruiting a challenge. It is more of a numbers game: you have to have a greater number of athletes in the recruiting pool, because of all the factors that come into play. The best candidates are strong students with a lot of financial need. The toughest kids to get are the solid students with little financial need. If they are not eligible for a lot of financial assistance and don't have the grades for the academic scholarships it makes it tough to offer them a good financial package. A lot of the decisions of the recruits come down to the financial aid package.

A high percentage of kids play at the Division III level because they can still play the sport they love and pursue their academic goals without as big of a time commitment as their peers at Division II and Division I schools. Plus, they often don't have the athletic skills to play at a higher level. That being said, it still takes a very good athlete to compete at the Division III level. My favorite part of coaching at this level is working with kids who are focused on school and their career path, which makes for rich, rewarding conversations. I believe academic and career pursuits should take priority over athletic commitments. Most of them are paying their own way to attend school, so they have a fundamental value of getting most out of their academic experience. Practice may have to take a backseat at times to the Organic Chemistry study session the professor is holding before the final. Those are the kinds of concessions Division III coaches often have to make, but I think it's a valid trade-off.

At the end of the day, these athletes are playing because they want to dedicate themselves and continue their career beyond high school. That takes dedication and commitment. As a coach, you get to work with athletes that have chosen to make that commitment. You may not have as much time to prepare for games—and therefore the planning may not be as in-depth—but you get to coach and teach and work with great young people.

Division I College Coaching

Division I takes everything to another level. The money that has been poured into collegiate athletics is mind-blowing: billions of dollars are spent annually on TV contracts for football and men's basketball. Women's basketball is third in line. The more money flowing through an athletic program, the greater the pressure to perform. The expectations and demands placed on coaches is incredible.

College football sets the tone for scrutiny. The incredible amount of airtime and revenue that football gets raises the expectations of the fans. It starts with the College Football Playoff schools—the bigger schools in the power conferences—and trickles down from there. The higher the level, the greater the paycheck, and the higher the expectations from the administration and the fans. Those coaches live under a microscope like few other people in the world.

In my experience, these outside influences can definitely have an impact on how coaches react in different situations. The "human factor" as I like to call it, has a tremendous effect on coaches. There are so many eyes upon what you are doing. The greater the exposure, the greater magnification of the microscope. If you get your identity from your coaching position, and not in your position with Christ, the pressure of public opinion will damage you from the inside out. First, it will eat your soul, then it will break down your vital organs. I've watched it happen in plenty of good coaches, myself included. Motivations vary greatly between coaches, but the truth about coaches is that we have big egos and love control. If we don't learn how to manage our need for control and get our hearts right, it can be the source of much pain.

Obviously, as coaches we want to win every game, but that's an extremely high bar to reach, no matter what level you coach. There must be a healthy balance between setting goals and expectations for your program that are challenging and realistic. The regular season positions your seed for the playoffs. Then it's a survive-and-advance mentality, with the end goal to win the championship. But in the end, only one team will win the championship, and every other team will drop off the chart, where they will face the wrath of their fans and sponsors.

The greatest challenge is managing people in your program. The staff needs to be supportive and functional to assist in the growth of the program, particularly the student-athletes. The athletes are your greatest asset to the program. It is the job of the staff to nurture and develop the athlete to be the best she can be for the program, but most importantly for the person she will become. The athletes at the Division I level are no different than athletes at the DII or DIII level, except for the fact that they likely are faster, stronger and have better skills. They likely have higher time demands placed on them by their coaches in return for the scholarship money they are receiving to compete. In turn, the pressure to perform can become more of an issue, requiring more guidance and support.

We coach because we love the game and the competition. The desire is to put your team in a position to win every game you play. At the DI level you are competing against the better competition, but the game is still the same. The competition is better and the stakes are higher. That is what adds to the fun in strategizing and preparing at a high level. The important thing is to keep things in perspective that it is a game, no matter what level. The athletes are just kids that are coming into your program. The ultimate goal is that they come to you to learn and grow and leave your program as better people, no matter what the tally is in the win column.

7

Life Lessons

TO THIS POINT in this book I have shared much about my coaching journey and have given you a window to the past that has brought me to the point of writing "Broken to Bold". I have gone through years of self-reflection and seeking guidance from others, but most importantly from the Holy Spirit. It has not always been fun – there have been many tears and tough realities that I have had to endure – but the good on the other side has been so worth it.

In this next chapter I would like to share many of the life lessons I have learned and need to continue to put into practice. You see, although I am in a good place, I still struggle a little bit with the loss of my career as a college basketball coach. I know it sounds strange to say that, after all the other progress I've made, but I see what women my age are accomplishing with their careers outside of the home. I am about to turn 50 as this book is getting ready to be published. This could likely be classified as a "mid-life crisis". I am at the point where my girls are more independent and less "needy". So, the question now comes in as to what shall I do with the increased amount of free-time I have.

When my coaching career ended, I moved into another phase of family life, with my greatest focus on being a mom and running our family "corporation." Is that still the right thing? Should I stay at home with my girls full time? I know that my most important job is to equip them to handle life's ups and downs and twist and turns better than I did. I have been working on planting the seeds of knowing God's grace, mercy, and love in their lives every single day so that they have their identity established in who they are and not what they do. Is that still to be my only focus?

Watching coaches on TV that I know from my coaching days resurfaced some feelings of self-doubt and comparison that really started to make me question the path I chose. At the same time, I see the fruit in my family life. I see my husband everyday expanding his footprint in his business (all glory to God for that) while I stay home and manage the household duties and take care of the kids. I am serving as the AD at the Catholic School my younger two attend and do basketball instruction a few hours a week, while coaching volleyball or basketball, depending on the season. This work is fulfilling, but I still fight my old demons of longing for approval from the outside world. It is a constant battle, but I know how to identify the attacks on my mind now and to fight them with the truth of the Word.

Psalm 139:14 says, "I praise you because I am fearfully and wonderfully made; your works are wonderful, I know that full well" (NIV). That is the truth. It helps me to fight the lies of the enemy that says that I need approval from others more than the approval of my Creator. The lies that try to keep me from "prospering where I am planted", in serving God by being faithful and diligent with where I am today as a wife, mom, coach, AD. I know that, and I fight it every day by staying close to the Word of God.

I share this with you to show that faith and trust in God

are not an endgame in and of themselves. It takes work every single day. The enemy does not rest. He smells when we are weak and vulnerable and will pounce like a lion. I need to daily sharpen my sword with the Word, which gives me strength daily to fight this battle, to teach my daughters and my athletes by my actions. When I fall in this area, I need to own it, confess it to them, apologize, and show through my own weakness that I need to get my strength from a higher power. We are not expected to live in perfection. Perfection is impossible. There is only one perfect ONE.

I encourage you to take action every single day to get to know God on a personal level, and to find your strength in Him. If you are already there, keep going. It is your job to teach that to the people over whom you have influence. It is the most important lesson you can teach them.

The following lessons are my gift to you. They are blessings I have received along the way to become stronger in Whose I am. May they help to strengthen you and to help you to be the best that you can be.

How Big Is Your God?

I heard this story today:

A father and son were sitting at the table one night. The boy asked his father, "Dad, how big is God?" His dad responded, "Son, look up that airplane in the sky. How big is it?" The boy responded, "It's tiny." So the dad took his son for a ride to the airport. The dad then said, "Son, how big is the airplane?" The boy responded, "It's gigantic." The dad smiled. "Son, God is like the airplane. The closer you get to Him, the bigger He gets."

Stay close to God and He will do big things in your life. Your wins and losses on the court won't seem so big. Focus on helping your players to grow into great members of society.

Teach them that life is bigger than basketball. Their job on this earth is to make it better, one decision at a time. With God at their side, it is a whole lot easier to get through this crazy life.

Who Is Your Personal Trainer?

Have you ever worked with a personal trainer—someone who was able to get more out of you than you ever thought you could do? If so, that person probably pushed you to the point of wanting to quit, but you stuck with it because:

- You were paying that person to push you past what you were capable of accomplishing on your own will
- You were getting results in your physical appearance, strength, agility, body fat, and energy levels
- The pain was worth it because you saw the results you achieved on the other side

In a similar way, we as coaches push our athletes through tough drills to build their skill, strength, and endurance. We make the practices harder than the games so that the game seems easy. We build the mental toughness to handle anything the opponent can throw at them in the heat of competition. We train them to overcome the grueling hours on the court with strength conditioning and a game plan to counter the opponent's effort on game day. It is through this training and refining of skills that we prepare them for victory.

I fell hard after getting let go at Akron. It was the lowest time in my life. I felt like a complete failure. I was embarrassed and ashamed. The exhaustion I felt day after day was like that feeling when you gave it all you had in a sprint workout, running 400's and puking in the infield grass, only to have to get up and do it again. (Did the coach think I signed up for track? Hello?) But seriously, my pain went so deep.

I let my assistants down. I let the athletes down. Others were hurting because of things that I had done. Was it intentional? No, but was it the truth? Yes. How do you recover from the magnitude of pain and hurt I was feeling, plus knowing that I had caused others to hurt as well? I needed to find a way to train myself out of this vortex of suffering. There was only one answer.

The answer is JESUS. He has a way of taking the pain and suffering—the times I have fallen so hard and didn't think I could get up, the puking-in-a-trash-can exhaustion— and turning it into a heroic testimony of good overcoming evil. Picture the scene in Wonder Woman, where she stands on the runway in the wake of destruction, having defeated her archenemy. That is how I feel when I stand with Jesus. My God is the master of causing good to triumph over evil.

This was not an easy process, by any means, but I took hold of the verse in Romans 8:1: "There is no condemnation to those who are in Jesus Christ, who do not walk according to the flesh, but according to the Spirit." I believed in God and Jesus before my huge fall, but I did not KNOW Him. I truly came to know what it meant to have a relationship with my Creator and to live in the Spirit. But now, knowing that my sins are washed clean, and my transgressions are forgiven has freed me of past pain. I fully understand that there are people in my life that won't forgive me for the pain I caused them, no matter how truly sorry I am. But I cling to the fact that because of the suffering of Jesus, I am forgiven. That was the turning point for me. I have been made new and refreshed. Where we fail, God sees the potential in our hearts and welcomes us to turn back to him. He knows the good. He knows our heart and can melt away the hardness that has developed. He turns hearts of stone to beat again in His love.

So, what does it mean to have Jesus as my personal trainer? He also comes with a helper, the Holy Spirit. The same Spirit that raised Him from the dead lives in me. That is the greatest gift - and it is FREE. I choose to train daily as I seek Him and lean into the Word for strength and endurance.

Maintain Control by Letting Go

Coaches LOVE control.

The need for control is so wired into our DNA that we don't know what to do when we are not in control. We control the players' time, workouts, schedules, behavior (or so we think). We control the outcome of the games by the calls we make in the games, which is why we despise the officials so much—they TAKE AWAY OUR CONTROL!

We are so egotistical and stubborn that we think the outcome of every game is the result of our preparation the night, days, or weeks before.

I'm right, aren't I?

Think about the crazy things you do as a coach to maintain at least the appearance of control:

- Those socks that you refuse to wash because you won while you were wearing them
- The way you fist-bump your assistants before the game—the same way in the same manner...EVERY SINGLE GAME
- Every superstition that you may think of that "affects the game"

The thing is, when we are winning, all of these crazy tricks "worked," but when we lose, it's because we should have run a different drill in practice... or the pregame shoot around wasn't EXACTLY how you planned it to go... or the other team screwed with you and put the balls out five minutes late at your shoot-around. Man, were you pissed. That HAD to be the reason you lost that game.

Coaches, we are CRAZY!! That control we so badly want to hold onto is what beats us up, day after day after day, leaving us feeling like we need everything to go as we plan it to go. Manipulating others in this way is really quite exhausting.

Are you with me?

What if a different perspective could bring more peace to your coaching life? What if this one simple paradigm shift could reorient the family life that you have been neglecting as you strive for a sense of control with your team? What if you could still coach and do other things that you love without damaging every other aspect of your life? The statistics are staggering. The divorce rate among Division I coaches is 67%. This statistic is PROOF that there are many coaches that are struggling just as I did. That is 2 out of 3 coaches. Think about that. If you are reading this and you are in the 33%, then chances are there are 2 coaches that you know that need to hear that there is a way to a better life. This stat blew my mind, but on the other hand was not shocking. I was on my way to that 67%. When I stopped coaching, my husband was so thankful to have "his girl" back. It breaks my heart to say it, but it is the truth. If you are on this path, please listen to the goodness that is on the other side of control. How, in letting go, you will have more control over the peace that you experience in your life.

Have you heard the expression "Let go and Let God"? You see, God doesn't care about your Win-Loss ratio—He cares about YOU. He can handle ALL that you have. He wants to give you peace and help you. You have to let go of the "wheel" and let Him steer. If you can grasp this, you will have the greatest win of your entire life. I am not saying that He is going to give you the perfect season just because you chose to let Him into your heart—ON and OFF the court, but it may give you more peace in your life.

On AND Off the Court

There are many Coaches who are Christians, believe in God, and go to church regularly. However, many of these coaches have double standards. They have an "at home" personality and an "at the office" personality, so they often aren't the same person with their team as they are at home. I hate to be the one to tell you, but you can't live this way forever and experience peace in your life.

Giving up your need for control leads to a more fruitful relationship with God, but it does not mean you lose everything. What you "lose" is the worry and fear that comes when you believe that every outcome rests solely on the decisions you make.

Imagine walking around with a 45-pound plate on your shoulders. You feel it weighing you down everywhere you go. Now, imagine how you would feel the moment someone lifted that weight off your shoulders. Can you feel it? Ahhhhh! That is what it feels like to give your worries over to Jesus. He is perfectly willing and able to carry that weight for you, all you have to do is ask Him and TRUST that He is with you. It's your choice to seek Him for answers to the challenges you are facing, and then trust that whatever happens is in the bigger plan. The hardest part, in all reality, is to allow yourself to rest in the belief that He has carved out a unique plan for you.

"For I know the plans I have for you, says the Lord, plans of peace and not evil, to give you a future and a hope," says

Jeremiah 29:11. His plans end up good. Now, the journey will not come without struggles and frustrations, but they will not involve carrying that 45-pound weight on your shoulders. When you find peace in trusting His promises, you will breathe easier and freer, every step of the way.

If you don't believe me, give it a try.

Take one area in your life that you grasp so tightly it hurts. Take that situation and give up the control to Jesus. He is already walking with you, so it's not like He's going out of His way to accommodate you. When you feel worry tightening like a noose around your neck because you don't know which way to go, simply take a deep breath. Close your eyes and ask Jesus to give you direction which way to go. Then quiet your mind until you feel peace about one of the options before you. He always guides us by peace. Whatever you feel the answer is after that, run with it. Make note of how you feel when you make that decision, and again when you reach the outcome, whatever that might be. You might be surprised at how peaceful you feel. Give it a chance. Try again. And again. And again. He will show you the way. "A man makes his plans, but the Lord guides his steps" (Proverbs 16:9).

Officials Are People, Too

"They're all awful."

"Officials suck."

"They never make the right call."

"They are out to get me."

"There's not a good official in the game."

If I had a dollar for every time I heard a coach or fan shout a line like this, I would be a trillionaire, for sure. As a coach, I was not always kind to officials, but I have to give a little credit to my mentors, Jodi, Mike, and Bill. They weren't exactly Pollyannas with the officials, either. You could say I learned how to get after the officials from the best of them. No blame, but it is true: you learn behaviors from those you work under, much like a child with a parent. Add to that my long-festering anger issues and you have a recipe for disaster.

Coaching at Akron was a tough road. We had to kick and claw for every basket. Every possession was a life-or-death struggle for me because I knew how outmatched we were. I always felt like I was playing 5-on-8. Of course, that is a completely ridiculous mindset to take into a game and I knew it, so I started each game with a positive, friendly approach. But at the first missed call, my alter ego came out, stamping my foot in a temper tantrum. You can probably picture it. Awesome, I know. I only had a couple of Technical Fouls in my career, as if that's any consolation, and I know there were worse coaches than me. That hardly makes it better.

Since my "retirement" from college coaching, I have coached over 200 youth basketball games in CYO (Catholic Youth Organization) and AAU (Amateur (American Athletics Union), and served as the Athletic Director, overseeing 30 coaches. I have been observing coaches' behavior on the sidelines, and have had to deal with coaches as an administrator. I hear the same negative comments about officials at every level. There must be something about a black-and-white striped shirt that brings out the worst in people.

True story: I was the Site Director for a sixth-grade CYO game. Seventeen- year-old Chad was a new official doing his first game in our gym, so I made a point to inform the coaches before the game that we had a new official and they should cut him slack. This was an "A-team" game, and these coaches were usually a bit more intense than the "B team" coaches. I told them to keep in mind that he was human and would do the best that he could. The Head Coach told me, "I will be sure to let my assistant know." I was satisfied that everything would be fine.

The match-up was St. William against St. Hilary, and I sensed from watching warm-ups that St. Hilary would have their hands full with that opponent. In the second quarter of a pretty physical game, St. William was up 12 points. St. William had the ball, but there was a tie-up, so their coach called a "timeout" to save possession. Chad blew the whistle and issued the time out, but did not signal a jump ball. He gave possession to St. Hilary. "It was a jump ball," Chad said.

Suddenly, a St. William Assistant Coach bellowed at the top of his lungs, "You gave us a time out! There can't be a jump ball and a time out!" Up and down the sideline, he stomped and barked, "There can't be a jump ball and a time out." That's when I intervened and told him to sit down and cool off. He should have gotten a Technical Foul, but Chad was young and probably feeling intimidated by this blustering "grown-up."

At halftime, I walked over to the bench and sat next to the Assistant Coach.

"Coach," I muttered quietly, "you were right about the call." He swiveled around and yelled into my face, "you need to tell me I'm right!"

"I just did."

Then he went off: "You need to tell him I'm right! Officials need to know the rules and they can't make mistakes! Once they put on that uniform, they can't make a mistake. We should be up on this team by 30 points!"

I'm not sure what I was thinking at that second, but I retorted, "and that's the official's fault." I shouldn't have said that, but I had let it fly and couldn't take it back. I tried to back-pedal as fast as I could to keep the assistant coach's wrath off of the official. "He's a young kid and he is human; he is going to make mistakes. Coach, this is sixth-grade basketball, so let's keep things in perspective." But by then, the coach was fully-committed to his rant and couldn't save face without seeing it through, saying, "I don't care about that, he can't make mistakes."

Mind you, this was sixth-grade basketball. What are we teaching our kids when we act this way as coaches? I have taken a good, hard look at the behavior of coaches and parents toward officials. Although that was an extreme example, it seems to be the opinion of coaches and fans that officials should be superhuman entities that cannot make mistakes. I agree that there are more officiating mistakes than there should be, but I have learned to hold my tongue and say very little to officials. Notice that I did not say, "say nothing" to officials. I am human, too, and I would be lying if I said I extended grace perfectly, but I have learned to keep things in perspective. One call usually does not make or break a game, and bad calls are evenly distributed to every team. I often say that officials are "equal-opportunity offenders."

At the end of the day, we have a couple of dozen kids playing a game. It's not multinational negotiations. Perspective is important. As coaches, we model how to respond to officials, and these kids model themselves after what they observe. Officials are fallible human beings, just like you and me. It is important to teach the kids not to make the officials a part of the game. Play the game, deal with the calls, and move on. Stay focused on the spirit of competition.

If It's Not Good, He's Not Finished

If you are not enjoying peace in your life—and you feel something is holding you back from being the best you can be—then it may be time to take the "leap of faith." There is such peace available when you release the striving and desire for control. If you don't have that peace, then He is not finished with you. Of course, He won't be totally finished with you until He calls you home. But He wants you to know that He is the Redeemer, the Waymaker, the Prince of Peace. He is Love, He is Peace, and He has work to do in you…if you will let Him in.

When adversity comes, God will cover you. He sees the good that can come from your pain. He is with you. He is for you. He will take your hand and walk through the river, the storm, and the fear with you. Fear will no longer master you. Control will no longer consume you. His love will do its perfect work in you.

Choose Love. Choose Him. He is with you ALWAYS.

"When you pass through the waters, I will be with
you; and through the rivers they do not over flow you.
When you walk through fire, you will not be scorched,
and the flame does not burn you." (Isaiah 43:2)

It's God's promise to you.

Life is our journey. We have desires and experiences in life that guide our decisions. God's promise is that He will be with us every step of the journey…If we invite Him to come along. The Holy Spirit is the guide that He has given to each of us. The Spirit only knows GOOD. Therefore, if we choose to walk with the Spirit the steps that He will guide us on are good.

My story I have shared with you is a living example of "If it's not good, He's not finished". My story on my coaching journey started out great. As life went on I made choices that did not always walk in the ways of the Spirit. That led to destruction in my career. It was not "good", but God was not finished. He took my pain and suffering over the past several years and has guided me back to Him. He used the bait of making money to bring me to the seminar, which opened my eyes to what was missing in my life: walking with Him. Now that I am walking with Him, this book is a testimonial of HIS GLORY. I had to take the leap of faith to write it. All Glory to God for the good that will be done in the name of Jesus through these pages.

"Break Me"

Each and everyone of us is broken in some way. We just don't always see what's right in front of us until it's too late. I had to get to the point of being totally broken before I was able to see what was missing in my life. I had hit the bottom. Fallen so hard that the only way to go was "to look up". Maybe you are not there...yet. Maybe you are having success on the court but your home life is fouling out, with a cracking marriage and shallow interactions with your kids. You put all of yourself into your job and give your family the leftovers. I've done that. I rationalized to myself that I would make it up in the off-season, but you and I both know the off-season never came. Your family might be suffering but you would never know, because you are not there with them, and when you are there, you're not really there.

Maybe you think you have a solid home life, but you are never home so you don't even know it. Your work life is so consuming that you are suffocating in the daily grind and the long hours. You are looking for the life-preserver, but the waves are so high you can't see it. Now might be the time to speak the simple prayer, "break me"—before life breaks you.

You don't have to wait for life to pull you completely under. God can help you, but you have to choose to allow Him to "break you"—to make the necessary changes in your life that will keep you from self-destructing. That's ultimately what He wants. He doesn't want to take away what matters most to you, but if you are clutching the wrong priorities and won't let go, he might need to "break you." It's really not a terrible thing, unless you fight it. Proverbs 29:1 says, "He who hardens his neck will be suddenly broken, and that without remedy". You don't want to get to that place, but if it comes down to having your favorite thing taken away or your life being completely shipwrecked, a merciful God would rather piss you off than let you be destroyed.

Yes, it really is that serious. Think about the shipwrecks you and I have seen in the coaching ranks. Do I need to name names? I think you understand.

Most people wait until it's too late; I'm urging you to reach out for help before you "think you need it." When life breaks you—whether in your job, your home, or relationships that you value—you find yourself facing difficult choices you shouldn't have to make. At that moment, you either choose to grow or to shrink. It's a painful experience, either way.

As uncomfortable and painful as "being broken" may sound, there is beauty in going willfully through it with God. On the other side of the pain and discomfort is an intimate, life-changing encounter with God: "[A]fter giving thanks, [Jesus] broke the bread and said, 'Take, eat, this is my body, which is broken for you; do this in remembrance of me'" (1 Corinthians 11:24, NIV). He was nailed to the cross and totally understands what it means to be broken. He understands everything you are going through, and will help you through it if you will invite Him. He followed His Father's will, carrying the cross to give us freedom in His brokenness. That gift is always there for us, but we have to choose to receive it.

"But, Kelly, I am comfortable in the life I have built for myself."

I hear you, friend.

You make a great salary and provide well for your family. They have everything they could possibly want. But let me ask you: do they have your presence in their lives, or is your life too full to fit them? Do you have peace and balance and wholeness in your life?

Perhaps the bigger question is, what do you lose by clinging to comfort? Comfort and prosperity and playing safe bring out the worst in us: complacency, fear of change, and fear of being uncomfortable. On the other hand, the best blessings are on the other side of the challenges and struggles that convict us to grow and stretch ourselves.

The reality is, when we are not broken (YET), we think we can handle things on our own. God knows YOU—He knows if you are on the verge of brokenness. He knows what keeps you up at night. It is so much more comforting to go to God. Instead of going it alone, or running to your "little g god," let the One True God break you down and build you up into exactly who He wants you to be. If you believe that you were created in your mother's womb by the Creator of the Heavens and the Earth, then you will find rest in going to Him with your brokenness, even if you don't think you will. "To be wholly useful to God, we have to be empty of self," says Craig Groeschel (Dangerous Prayers, page 70)—empty of the selfish desires that hold us back from being the best we can be in all we do.

"But Kelly, I already know God."

I thought I did, too.

I was a good church-going girl, faithful to show up at mass every weekend, but I have since learned that, no matter where you are in your relationship with Jesus, there is ALWAYS room to grow, just as there is in any relationship. I have been married to Todd for 18 years. We started out with what we thought was a good relationship. After all, we never had arguments and things were usually comfortable. I'd say that's pretty good. Good enough, anyway.

Recently, we attended a marriage seminar and got

smacked upside the head about things that we thought were good:

If you are not arguing, or at least disagreeing on things, then your communication is not going very deep. OUCH!

There were hurtful things from our past that we had buried deep and that needed to come out. Often these are little things that we ignore or push aside that fester and pile up over the years. We don't deal with them and they become a wedge that slowly separates. You don't even know that wedge is there, it is so subtle. We were prompted to identify these issues. Each was painful to uncover and discuss, but identifying and addressing them brought forgiveness and healing which has brought us even closer together.

Our marriage is better than it's ever been because we chose not to be satisfied with "good enough."

Your relationship with God is like a marriage. I have been in this "marriage" with Jesus for six years and I am still discovering new things every day about His love, grace, and mercy. We get deeper in our relationship as He reveals things that I don't know about Him and the places in my heart and soul that need healing. It is an ongoing process, but in my weakness I continue to see the strength of God shining through my life. He is so good and patient and loving. It is an amazing journey.

As Craig Groeschel says in *Dangerous Prayers* (page 75), "We don't know what blessing is on the other side of God's breaking."

Overcoming

There are actually blessings on the other side of the pain, failures, and setbacks in life. You can't experience real success without encountering obstacles you must overcome. This is the normal path of success. It is usually in working through the challenges and getting to the other side that the true reward comes. Think of your team. Have you ever had a conflict among the players? Silly question, right? In addressing and resolving the conflict did you find that your team was stronger after tackling that conflict? Conflict creates room to heal and to grow. This is true in the spiritual breaking as well.

When we surrender to God all that we are and ask Him to reveal in us what needs to change—we are asking Him to break us. On the other side of this breaking, we find the blessing: healing for wounds we have suffered in the past, strengthening through faith, and greater compassion for the plight of others. As you learn to trust God above all else, He will heal your heart to fully love others. Ultimately, in being broken, we can be made whole in mind, body and spirit, living in strength from our Heavenly Father.

In humbling ourselves, we are actually made stronger.

A New Thing

"See I am doing a new thing. Now it springs up; do you not perceive it? I am making a way in the wilderness and streams in the desert." (Isaiah 43:19 NIV)

Incidentally, I've been to those streams. In March of 2019, on my trip to Israel, I had the opportunity to visit En Gedi, the actual place Isaiah was talking about in that verse, and step into those crystal waters. There was a waterfall in the middle of the desert. It is quite beautiful.

Just as God can make a waterfall in the desert, He can make new things in your heart. Have you ever seen a raw diamond? It starts out as an ugly piece of rock. The jeweler's process is to chisel away at it, bit-by-bit, persistently refining and uncovering the magnificent beauty inside. It takes a lot of work, but the result is well worth the effort. Looking back at my mistakes was my chiseling. Most of the time, I hated the process, but I had to go through the pain to get to the richness on the other side.

Think about the things you want to change about yourself. The fact that you got this far in this book tells me that you want something more than what you are experiencing today. You are hanging on because there is something nagging at you: you know you need to make a change, and you are willing to take the necessary steps so you can enjoy a better life and career. If you aren't quite sure why you are still here, I encourage you to ask. Don't ask me or your spouse; close your eyes and ask Him. He is a loving Father Who wants nothing more than to help you.

If you are ready to start on a new path, to break free from the things holding you back from being the best YOU in EVERY area of your life, keep on reading and get ready to take action. This next part will help you get started, but then it will be time for you to activate all those great characteristics that got you into coaching in the first place: perseverance, determination, focus. I know you have what it takes to achieve everything you want in life, no matter how difficult the changes might be.

The first step in this process is getting to know the One who made you and planted the great desire in you to coach and lead. It's simply building a relationship—you already know how to do it. You have done it with your players, your staff, and your recruits, and—if you're lucky enough to be married—with your spouse and kids. You spend time with them, and that is exactly what you need to do with God. We get to know Him through spending time reading His word.

The more we know God's word, the more we know God; The more we know God, the more we will TRUST Him.

Epilogue
SO, WHERE DO WE GO FROM HERE?

AT THIS POINT, I wouldn't be a good coach if I didn't extend a challenge to help you develop your game. After all, I'm guessing you came to this book because you wanted to take your skills as a coach to the next level in some meaningful way. I hope you feel you are walking away with something more.

So, let me guide you through the process I took to find healing. I want you to get really honest with yourself as you consider the following questions:

1. Where do I get my identity? Am I defined by what I do or by Who I am?
2. Who am I?
3. Is God the center of my life?
4. Are my priorities in this order?

    A. God
    B. My spouse
    C. My kids
    D. My work

5. What do I idolize?

   A. Money (am I consumed with making money)?
   B. Work (do I put work first above my family)?
   C. Stuff (car, house, electronics)?
   D. Other people's opinions?
   E. Netflix?
   F. Sports?
   G. Other?

6. What needs to change in me?

As you go through this, take time to thank God for who He made you to be. Ask God to help you search your heart as you answer these questions. Ask for the wisdom and guidance of the Holy Spirit to wash over you as you work on self-discovery.

Are You Missing the Point Of Coaching?

Do you seek the freedom to be that carefree, fun-loving coach you once were, or are you stuck in the rut of the "win at all costs" mentality so deep that you can't see your way out? You might be winning games, but you are empty because you know something is missing.

If you are coaching for the wrong reasons, like the approval of man, then you are completely missing the true glory in what you are doing. You are missing the best part of this game called life. If God is not the center of all you are, then the victories are simply a short-term one-liner in your story. I speak out today in boldness of the greatness of my God and how His love, grace, and mercy have gotten me to this point in my life.

Getting fired, having the most important thing in my life

taken away, was the best thing that happened to me. I was liberated from the idol of coaching Division I college basketball that consumed my being. An "idol" is whatever occupies your mind and becomes your god. I suffered from a bad case of idolatry to the basketball god. My identity was "coach" and everything else in my life revolved around it. It was more important than my marriage. God loved me so much that He woke me up from my trance.

If you are in a "trance" of "winning is everything", I encourage you to step back and look in the mirror. It's not too late to turn things around. You are called to coaching. You have been given the gift and the appointment to lead others through your sport. What a blessing that is. Ask yourself, what am I doing this for? If you are struggling with that answer, there may be some heart issues that you need to deal with. If you are winning and are fighting this then chances are that others around you are feeling the same thing, open up and discuss. If you are losing and having these feelings, open up and discuss, find a trusted friend who can help you. If you need a trusted friend, reach out to me. I would be honored to help you change that reflection in the mirror.

Mirror Check

Looking in the mirror and being honest with yourself is not always the easiest thing to do. Looking at that reflection and being transparent with others is even harder. This may be helpful to you, so here it goes. Even though I know all of this good stuff, and continue to grow in my ability to be the Christ-like leader I am called to be, I still struggle with walking the walk. I have to check myself every game. Sometimes, other coaches do things that trigger my competitive nature and I lose sight of my mission. It's the human factor, and it forces me to reflect on the Amazing Grace of our God and how I need to extend that same grace to others.

Just yesterday, I had two games: one fifth-grade game and one seventh- grade game. The fifth-grade team played a pretty good team that had a few girls that were very strong defensively. In fifth grade, you can run some sets and get kids into the paint to make a few shots here and there, but a team with a couple of good defenders can thwart your efforts pretty quickly. That makes for a long game. I found myself getting very frustrated with a few of my players. I have to check myself, because I have greater expectations of the girls as the season rolls on. That's normal for any coach. The frustration comes in when the girls don't execute the plays we have practiced over and over again, and then make the same mistakes over and over again. My own ego rears its little head as I fear that people will think that I don't know what I am doing – Yes, this even happens when I am coaching 5th graders - that I didn't teach them to back cut when denied on the wing and to pass-fake when the defender is in the passing lane. The turnovers mount and the mistakes lead to easy baskets. A point differential is really hard to make up in fifth grade. That's when I start to "over-coach", call timeouts, draw up special situations, and confuse them more than they already are. That's when I leave the gym in frustration because I lost sight of what we are supposed to be doing. I have to check myself and come to the next practice focusing on why we are here and what youth sports is about. It is a constant process and extremely humbling.

I would like to offer encouragement to you if you are coaching young kids and face some of these same feelings. It is natural to have feelings of frustration in coaching. Remember why the KIDS are there – to have fun! They don't carry losses away from the game as much as some parents do. Focus on the effort and not the outcome. Be the encourager and cheerleader on the sidelines. The goal is to keep them coming back, gaining that desire for teamwork and physical activity. If you are fortunate enough to "get to" coach your son or daughter and his or her friends that is a complete gift. Embrace it and remember that it is "not about you", that person in the mirror, it is WAY bigger than that!

> # Overtime
> OTHER THOUGHTS FROM A COACH'S PERSPECTIVE

Landmarks Are Opportunities to Reflect

As I approach this landmark birthday, I continue to reflect on life:

- What do I value?
- What influences do I allow to speak into my life?
- What feelings and emotions do I listen to?
- Most importantly, where is my God in all of this?

I stopped working on this book for about a month because I got caught up in the thoughts and doubts in my head: "What if no one reads my book? "Who am I to think I can write a book?" "Am I really worthy of this?" "Who is this for?"

Then I read this morning's devotion from *Jesus Calling* by Sarah Young:

> "If you live your life too safely you will never know the thrill of seeing me work through you. When I gave you My

> *Spirit, I empowered you to live beyond your natural ability and strength."*

This was inspired by Galatians 5:25, which says, *"Since we live by the Spirit, let us keep in step with the Spirit."*

This really hit home for me. If I live too safely, too comfortably, not stretching myself to get out of my comfort zone, then I am not allowing the unlimited potential and the hand of God to shine in His glory through all that He can accomplish in me. If this work is truly inspired by God and a work for His glory, then He will bless it beyond my imagination. This is not for me, but for those that may need to be encouraged by my failures. Those who need to be inspired to get up, rise up, and do something beyond what they ever dreamed they could do.

I never dreamed of writing a book until the seed was planted in me a few years ago when I started to share my testimony of how God was working in my life—a transformation that may help others to see that their life is important to our Father and Creator. He wants to do good works through each of us, but we have to allow Him to do so by accepting the challenges He puts before us.

Being Who We Are

I am a wife, mom, daughter, sister, friend, coach, teacher, encourager, warrior, lover, fighter, bold, courageous, kind, funny, a good listener, wise, understanding, woman of great faith, child of the Most High. I went from sinner to forgiven, failure to overcomer, prideful to humble, abandoned to adopted, selfish to selfless. All of this I have discovered by the grace of God. This is not the end of my road, just the beginning and will take work to stay on that road.

I have spent the last six years working on myself. My

journey started out to learn to make more money because that would surely be the answer to my problems. That was the "bait" to get me to "First Steps to Success" where I was first brought to my knees in front of my Heavenly Father. What I found was that money did not solve my problems. What I needed most was to find my true self once again; the fun-loving, confident, fun, energetic, enthusiastic kid who had no fear, looked out for others, encouraged and protected those that I loved. The biggest truth that I discovered was that God created me, as He has created each of us, in His own image. His love for me goes deeper than I can humanly imagine. He is a forgiving and loving God. He has forgiven me for my past mistakes as the Bible says, "as far as the east is from the west my sins are remembered no more." The shame that I felt from being fired for my shortcomings and lack of success at Akron has been wiped away.

I have learned to dig deep into myself and to identify who I am so that I can live a confident and fulfilled life. The way God designed me with the ability to teach and coach and encourage others. He designed me with these gifts. He made me a woman of strength and conviction. I am wired to take on new challenges with the purpose of making situations better. I am bold in my faith. I use my past experiences and what I have learned about the love of our Heavenly Father to teach middle-school kids how important it is to develop a relationship with God and tie it in with their sports experiences. I love to work with kids and help them gain confidence in who they are on and off the field of competition. I teach basketball skills to many individual athletes from middle school to high school helping them to improve on their ball handling skill and shooting technique but most importantly help them become stronger people physically and mentally.

I am a wife and mother and a woman of strong faith. I am a mom who loves her husband and daughters beyond measure. I continue to work on myself to be a great wife and to teach my girls that we are all works in progress. By example, I continue to learn and grow and teach them the importance of being teachable and humble in all they do. I am blessed to be their coach in grade school basketball-coaching is coaching at any level. Coaching and teaching and nurturing them along with their friends is my greatest reward. It is an amazing gift for me to be able to spend time helping them develop.

My Life Is Not My Own

This spring has been tough. The flu hit our house hard. As I am sitting here writing, it has been 25 straight days of illness in my house. I was down for the count for about eight days, where I didn't do much besides watch a lot of movies and a lot of basketball. The cool thing is that I got to spend time with my daughter, Finley, as we were laid out at the same time. Good thing that she is a basketball-watching junkie, too. She and I spent a lot of time watching women's college basketball and talking about game situations. It was actually pretty awesome.

The problem for me arose as I had a lot of time to think. What if I would have jumped back into coaching after getting fired rather than taking the year off? What if I would have stuck with it -- where would I be today? I was suffering from a case of FOMO, or the Fear of Missing Out. What did I miss out on by choosing to walk away from college coaching? It is really a tough place to be emotionally as I approach this midlife milestone.

Last night, I was watching the beautiful celebration of the lives of Kobe and Gigi Bryant. Talk about getting a punch-in-the-gut reality check! I listened to Vanessa eulogize her 13-year-old daughter and the experiences she would not get to have with her. What a sweet, loving daughter she was, and what life will be like without those milestone experiences of high school graduation, and a wedding with her daddy walking her down the aisle. I was captivated by her words about Kobe, the husband and father, not Kobe the basketball player. Basketball is what he did, and everyone knows it; but who he was as a man, a father, a husband, a coach, a mentor and an encourager has been lost in the abrupt, premature end of his life.

Geno Auriemma spoke, as well—not about Kobe as a basketball player, but about his role as Gigi's doting dad. That was his number one focus. How they loved the game of basketball, and how he took her to the University of Connecticut to plant the seeds of her future. That made me look at my life in sharp relief.

In that moment, I realized that my life is not my own anymore. Once I became a mother, that became my most important role. My priorities shifted from chasing my own dreams to helping each one of my daughters realize their dreams. I had my time to pursue my career in coaching. I made the choice to not get back into the circle of college coaching. I chose to be a mom first and to have my coaching gigs on the side.

My first team is my husband and three amazing daughters. This is where the most important coaching gets put into practice: guiding, mentoring, challenging and encouraging them to discover and follow their dreams.

My second team is the kids I coach through the school and AAU, my Champion Athletes for Christ group, the coaches I guide as Athletic Director. I am making a difference in the lives of young people. It isn't on the big stage; it's in the local gyms and classrooms.

My life is not my own. I am a tool for my Heavenly Father to use to enrich His kingdom on earth. It is my daily mission to "...encourage one another, and build up one another, as indeed you do," as Paul directs us in 1 Thessalonians 5:11. I want to continue to live as I heard Pastor Steven Furtick say in a sermon:

> *"...to be responsible to produce what's in (me). Right now, the Kingdom of God is with (me). I want to be blessed like the Bible says "blessed." I want to be happy where I'm at. I want God to bring forth the fruit that He put in me. I will not quit on the fruit he gave me because I do not see it in the sensational way. I am free from the need for the approval of people, to have the approval of God, not fame and all the follows. If the Kingdom is within (me) it can not be taken away....God wants us to get Heaven on Earth."*

And so, I ask myself, am I getting it right? Am I being the best mom, wife, sister, daughter, friend and coach I can be?

What questions are you asking yourself today?

So Much More To Say

I have so much more I'd like to add to this section; more stories and illustrations keep bubbling up to the surface as I sit here, and I certainly haven't learned all the useful lessons from these memories. But at some point, I need to hand this over to the editor and send it off for publishing. That said, I'd like to invite you to join me in an ongoing conversation. I'm sure you have things growing in your heart that you want to talk about. I'd love to hear it.

So, you bring a cup of coffee and I'll bring mine, and let's see what our Father wants to show us next.

You Are Invited!

If you have experienced brokenness and have found some healing in this book, please consider sharing it with others. It is through your pain and testimonial that others are set free from their bondage, brokenness, and pain. Someone may have chains broken off their life because you have the courage to share.

Feel free to reach out to *coachkellykennedy@gmail.com* to receive prayers and encouragement.

Resources

These are the sources I have used to strengthen my faith and have helped contribute to the content of this book:

Books:

Dangerous Prayers, by Craig Groeschel
Shepherd Coach, by Tom Roy

Seminars:

First Steps to Success business seminar, Dani Johnson (danijohnson.com)
Play Like a Champion Today—playlikeachampion.org

Online Resources:

Revelation Wellness – Whole in Mind, Body and Soul - Revelationwellness.org
Proverbs 31 Ministries

Thank You

I want to thank all the coaches that have helped me through the years:

- Mr. Braddock, Mr. Williams, Mr. Timko, and (of course) my Uncle Ed, for helping me to develop as a young player and giving me the opportunity to play the game I love.
- Thank you to Maureen Kirby Becker, "Kirbs", my high school coach, for being an ear to me off the court (as well as a great teacher on the court), for giving me my first coaching jobs at Regina High School, and for going way above and beyond as you and Brian took me to visit college campuses to explore my future and were there to guide me along the way.
- Thank you to Carol Dugan for believing in me, giving me the opportunity to play college basketball, and helping me to get started in my coaching career.
- Thank you to all the coaches that included me on their staffs and helped to groom me to reach my dream of becoming a Division I Head Women's Basketball Coach: Ronda Seagraves, Glada Munt, Jody Runge, Mike Petersen, and Bill Fennelly.
- Thank you, Mike Thomas, for inviting me into your inner circle at The University of Akron.
- And thank you for all the coaches that I have worked with, laughed with, coached camp with, traveled with and gotten bleacher bum with through the years. You have touched my life along my journey—there are so many. I am grateful for each of you.

My Apologies

To my players at the University of Akron: I did not give you the experience you deserved as a college athlete while I was fighting my own battles. May you find it in your heart to forgive me. Know that I am deeply sorry for any hurt that I caused you. I was missing a very important relationship in my life at that time. As I have come to know my Creator, my heart and mind have been made new. As He has done for me, I pray that He works out all for good for you. Even in our trials, His mercy, grace, and love shine through. To my coaching staff at Akron as well: I was not a great leader in bringing us all together to work for a common goal. I have learned a great deal since then and I am sure you have as well. May you find it in your heart to forgive me for my lack of leadership of our staff.

Acknowledgments

I would like to thank my Mom for her unwavering faith through the years. There is no doubt in my mind that her prayers helped to keep me out of real trouble and kept the grace of God as my protector. The power of prayer is real.

Thank you to my editor, Chad Ketcher, for doing an amazing job of helping me craft my thoughts and experiences into a book. You have an amazing gift, my friend.

For the support and encouragement of my friends and family to continue to write this book. For all those that took the time to read the unpolished copy and provide insights, especially Tina W., Bill F., Steph N., Katie A., Tom R., and Kristin S. You helped me to smooth out the rough edges. Your help is much appreciated and your friendship cherished.

KELLY KENNEDY has been in coaching for almost 30 years. She spent 13 years coaching basketball at the college level. Her stops included assistant coaching positions at Southwestern University, the University of Oregon, Texas Christian University (TCU), Iowa State University and culminated at the University of Akron, where she served as Head Women's Basketball Coach. As she continues to coach youth sports and do private instruction, her main focus is the mental and spiritual development of athletes and coaches. Kelly and her husband, Todd, live in Copley, Ohio with their three amazing daughters.

For more information visit:
CoachKellyKennedy.com

email // **coachkellykennedy@gmail.com**

 twitter.com/CoachKelKen

Endnotes

Introduction

1. Words and Music by MATT CROCKER, JOEL HOUSTON & SALOMON LIGTHELM © 2012 Hillsong Music Publishing (APRA). All rights reserved. International copyright secured. Used by permission

Made in the USA
Middletown, DE
09 December 2020

27040673R00120